And He Taught Them With Pictures

D1613569

And He Taught Them With Pictures:

The Parables in Practice Today

Josef Imbach

TEMPLEGATE  PUBLISHERS

Originally published in German as
Und Lehrte Sie In Bildern
by Echter Verlag Würzburg in 1995

English translation by Jane Wilde © 1997 by
Templegate Publishers

Templegate Publishers
302 East Adams Street
P.O. Box 5152
Springfield, IL 62705
(217) 522-3353
http://www.templegate.com

ISBN 0-87243-226-2
Library of Congress Catalog Number:
97-60411

CONTENTS

Introduction

When there is talk of parables most Christians probably think of the Bible, particularly the New Testament. It seems to be not widely known that the simile or parable was one of the most popular literary forms in early Jewish writings. Therefore it should be no surprise to learn that these stories also have a firm place in the Talmud,[1] in which the religious traditions of Judaism are laid down in writing. An example?

As R. Isaak and Rab Nachman took leave of each other, Rab Nachman said to his friend:

"Master, bless me!"

And he answered him: "I want to tell you a parable. What does this remind you of? A man went into the desert, and was hungry, tired and thirsty. And he found a tree whose fruit was sweet, whose shade was pleasant, and under this tree flowed a water course. He ate of its fruit and drank of its water, and sat in its shade. And when he was ready to go, he said: 'Tree, Tree! With what can I bless you? If I should say to you: your fruit is sweet — it is already sweet!

Your shade is pleasant — it is already pleasant! May a water course flow beneath you — it flows already! Rather it is the will of God that all your shoots that we plant out should be as you are!'

It is just like that with you (said R. Isaak to Rab Nachman). With what shall I bless you? With knowledge of the Torah? You have it already. With riches? You have them already. With sons? You have them already. It is far more God's will that your children should be as you are"![2]

Naturally many opinions about teaching and numerous legal requirements are expressed in the Talmud. However, in contrast to Christian theology, the Jewish teachings on faith do not present an organized system of abstract dogmas, but are mainly concerned with discussions, debates, wise sayings, cases of law, and also with the workings of God in this world and in the destiny of mankind seen through legends and stories of miracles. Judaism on the whole prefers narrative to dogma. Of course there are also a number of Jewish scholars of divinity who have written theological tracts. You only have to remember Josef Caro (1488-1575) whose work "Sculcham Aruch" (The Laid Table, 1565) still serves orthodox Jews today as the legal basis of rules on community matters. But no less than this and other standard works, the pious Jew values the countless stories of examples and devotional episodes, or the profound anecdotes that have been passed down, often over hundreds of years. This does not only apply to the haggadic (recited) texts, but also to the Halachah, which describes the legal requirements of Talmudic wisdom that are concerned with the ethical behavior of mankind.

Although Thomas Aquinas (c. 1225-1274) in whole chapters of his "Summa Theologica" *reflects* upon God's characteristics, the Talmud (and indeed the Hebrew Bible) represents these characteristics by *telling* us what God has brought about in the past, and how He continues to work on in the lives of men. And while Alphonsus Liguori (1696-1787) splits hairs all over the place in his attempts to define the fluid barriers between guilt and innocence a little more sharply, the Talmud *reports* on hundreds of decisions — some of them really contradictory — that Jewish religious scholars hit upon in the past.

"Plunge boldly into life; Enjoy it to the full"
(Goethe, Faust, Prologue for the Theater)

Jesus the Jew is also entirely committed to the tradition of his Jewish religious community. It is therefore not surprising that he constantly illustrates his instructions with stories in which the daily lives and the dreams and desires of his fellow countrymen, as well as his own ideas and teaching, are reflected.

The protagonists in these stories are recruited from all social strata. The talk is of perfectly ordinary peasants, shepherds, housewives, of rich landowners and their tenants, of despairing believers and of debtors wringing their hands. Kings and squires tread the boards along with clever business people, day wagers and idlers who avoid work, sleepy headed bridesmaids, and a cunning scoundrel who deceives a great landowner twice. At first we may smile at them, but finally they make us reflect. Some stories thrive on contrast: people who keep their distance from each other in life suddenly find themselves cheek by jowl, like the tax collector and the Pharisee who meet in the temple and are yet miles apart from each other; or the rich glutton and the beggar Lazarus who only realizes in heaven that *he* has hit the jackpot; or like the temple priest, a strict believer, and the heretical Samaritan who cannot even quote from a single ecumenical edition of the holy scriptures in a disputation. Further episodes give us a colorful view of family relationships and social customs

9

of the time. They tell of the conflicts between fathers and sons, of distressed widows and bribable judges, of capricious children and importunate friends, of opulent feasts and cheerful village weddings. Even evil spirits and demons are called up; in those days the people's fantasy was no less aroused by them than it is today by parapsychology and science fiction. Jesus continually falls back upon events in nature: a sower, a tiny mustard seed, a parched fig tree and weeds in the field of corn inspire him to tell stories that one cannot disregard because they linger in the mind.

The gospels portray Jesus as an exciting story teller, a poor wandering preacher and poet, animated by his desire to pass on his message to other people, to move them to repentance, and to proclaim God's forgiveness and His kingdom. His stories give us vivid pictures which fill such a broad canvas that we are able to reconstruct the whole of the good tidings from them alone.

Like the rabbis of his time, Jesus also made use of various types of parables. Some of these belong to the literary genre of stories that *teach or give example,* which draw the listeners' attention to modes of action that can either be imitated, or that serve as a deterrent. In these teachings Jesus wants to give us suggestions for practical behavior; remember the story of the Pharisee and the tax collector (Lk. 18, 10-14), of the rich glutton and poor Lazarus (Lk. 16, 19-31) or the story of the good Samaritan (Lk. 10, 29-37).[3]

In contrast, Jesus's *actual similes* are concerned with quite normal events, which, precisely because of their mundane character, have an exemplary significance. There is the woman who loses a drachma and sweeps out her whole house (Lk. 15, 8-10). Then there is the shepherd who loses a sheep and goes off to find it (Lk.15, 4-7). If Jesus afterwards draws a comparison with God, his people understand what is meant at once, because in this case they themselves would have behaved in exactly the same way.

Apart from this, Jesus also created quite a number of *parables*. A parable is a story that describes a unique event; this contributes to a heightening of tension. A landowner's paying all his workers the same wages, although some of them had only worked for an hour, would surely have been an unusual occurrence at the time of Jesus (Mt. 20, 1-16). And it would surely not have been the order of the day for a few rebellious grape pickers to kill some of the servants and then the only son of a vineyard owner. (Mk. 12, 1-9).

Finally, several of Jesus's similes and parables show great similarities with the literary genre the *allegory* (from the Greek *alla agoreuein* = to say something else, to speak in images). A classic example of this is the story of the Sower (Mk. 4, 1-9). At first sight, we seem to be *actually* dealing with a *simile*; an entirely mundane event is depicted. But the careful reader will notice that a specific and pertinent meaning is assigned to each element in the story (sower, seeds, path, birds eating seeds, rocky ground, thorn bushes, good soil):

"The Sower *sows* the word. And these are the ones *along the path where the word is sown;* when they hear, *Satan immediately comes* and takes away the word *which is sown in them. And these in like manner are the ones sown upon* rocky ground, *who, when they hear the word, immediately receive it with joy; and* they have no root in themselves, but endure for a while; *then, when tribulation or persecution arise on account of the word, immediately they fall away. And others are the ones sown* among thorns; *they are those who hear the word, but* the cares of the world, *and the delight in riches,*

and the desire for other things enter in and choke the word, *and it proves unfruitful. But those that were sown upon* good soil are the ones that hear the word and accept it and bear fruit, *thirtyfold and sixtyfold and a hundredfold" (Mk. 4, 14-20).*

In the allegory each individual feature of the imagery refers to a hidden meaning that has to be brought out (the seed stands for the word of God, the sower for Jesus etc.) The actual meaning is hidden behind what is said in the allegory, and it is obviously difficult to approach it. According to Mark's gospel, Jesus chides his own disciples because they are incapable of fathoming for themselves the significance of the images that he uses: "Do you not understand this parable? How then will you understand all the parables"? (Mk. 4, 13). Afterwards he explains the deeper meaning of his language to them himself. There is no further need to emphasize the fact that the sower means Jesus.

However this conclusion was not so urgent for Jesus's disciples. Today researchers are almost without exception of the opinion that although the parable of the sower goes back to Jesus himself, its allegorical interpretation was put into his mouth by the evangelists.

Every Tradition Requires Interpretation

There are many good reasons to support this assumption. It is known that the gospels are not records like court transcripts: we are not concerned with historical documents in the modern sense. The evangelists also tell us how Jesus lived and what he taught. But at the same time they allow their own experiences with the resurrected Jesus within their communities to blend into the story. In other words, they do not distinguish between fact and commentary.

Here is an illustration of what that means. Let us suppose there has been a terrible traffic accident. A newspaper would give the details of what had happened, the number of dead and injured, and the extent of the resulting damage. A description given by an eye witness would have been quite different. Inevitably the experience of the horror he had survived would be expressed in his account. And again a priest would speak quite differently about this accident in his Sunday sermon. The circumstances in which it all happened are now no longer in the foreground; in the first place the priest would probably want to remind us that there is no moment in our lives when we are safe from death.

To some extent the evangelists can be compared to this priest. Their main intention is not to deliver the bare facts. The objective in their writings is far more to proclaim Jesus as the Redeemer. Naturally in doing this they also bring up their own experiences of belief.

In addition, the situation of their readers, the people for whom they were preparing their records, is constantly before their eyes during the writing of their books. Faithful to the spirit of Jesus, they seek to give an answer to new questions which concern the proclamation and practice of faith, and also the organizational questions of the early Christian communities. In concrete terms this means that the evangelists do not simply hand down Jesus's message word by word, but always relate it to their present circumstances and interpret it.

For instance, a christological high point characterizes the parable of the marriage feast in *Matthew* (22, 1-10) because the evangelist refers the parable in an allegorical way to Jesus's destiny. *Luke* on the other hand, (14, 16-24) uses it as an example of the right behavior towards those in need.[4] In the face of such interpretations the question arises as to how Jesus himself told his parables.

It is probable that the original form of this parable can be reconstructed by first comparing the various written records of the individual evangelists with each other, and then working out their mutual elements. Besides, each time one must call to mind the teaching opinions of Jewish theology that Jesus refers to in his entire proclamation, either agreeing with them, correcting them or dismissing them. Finally, the current social customs that he constantly returned to must be taken into account.

We must also not underestimate the fact that there is a sociological barrier to understanding because Jesus lived in a world and culture that are totally foreign to us. This alone makes the approach to his parables difficult, and for this reason in my book I have drawn repeatedly upon modern literary texts that reflect insights and experiences which make it easier to cross the bridge from today to those times.

Parables: a Stimulus to Theology

One cannot imagine Jesus's preaching without the parables. Mark emphasizes that Jesus "with many such parables.... spoke the word to them, as they were able to hear it" (Mk.4,33). Matthew takes up this statement and even maintains (supported by a verse from a psalm) that Jesus "...said nothing to them without a parable" (Mt. 13,34; see Ps. 78,2). The fact is that the parables are the bedrock of Jesus's preaching.

It is therefore all the more astonishing that they hardly play a part in the textbooks of dogmatic and moral theology, not to mention canon law. They have their firm place in popular preaching and catechesis.

On the other hand in theology they have nothing like the value that Jesus placed upon them.

On the whole it seems that theologians fall back upon this or that parable occasionally, when they wish to illustrate or support a particular teaching opinion (they refer particularly to the parable of the Kingdom of God).[5] In other words, dogmatists and moral theologians seem to take Jesus's individual parable stories into account only when they are unavoidable, and to the extent that they fit into the framework of their previously given system of teaching.

This book takes the opposite direction. The parables will not be read through the spectacles of systematic theologians, but will be examined for the anthropological knowledge and theological insights they can pass on to us. We are not aiming primarily at expanding theological knowledge, but at deepening and enlivening faith.

I would like to thank Frau Imelda Casutt for correcting the proofs. She gave up a considerable amount of her free time, and found many mistakes that I had overlooked on the computer. I would also like to thank Dr.Michael Lauble for the careful way he edited this book.

1
The Substance of Jesus's Preaching

A great number of the many stories that Jesus told converge upon one theme: God's magnanimity and goodness towards men. He emphasizes not only how much store God sets by each individual human being, but that it is precisely the moral failures and those we call losers who can be certain of His devotion. To an extent these stories comprise the substance of his whole teaching. Obviously Jesus told these stories so frequently because he considered everything else as self-evident.

We seem to believe that God, according to the Hebrew Bible, takes merciless revenge for every fault; and he must take revenge, because otherwise his righteousness would be at stake. For the same reason every good deed is inevitably followed by a reward from this God. The greater the achievement, the greater the wages; the worse the offense, the harder the punishment. The relationship between man and God is predominantly determined by the law of retaliation.

The view that every sin must be atoned for runs like the dominant theme through all the Old Testament writings; and Jesus calls these to mind again and again. A well-known example of this is the story of the flood.

"The Lord saw that the wickedness of man was great in the earth, and that every imagination of the thoughts of

his heart was only evil continually. And the Lord was sorry that he had made man on the earth, and it grieved him to his heart. So the Lord said, 'I will blot out man whom I have created from the face of the earth, man and beast and creeping things and birds of the air, for I am sorry that I have made them.'" (Gen. 6,5-7)

Disease, suffering, death, in short all evil always appears in the early sections of the Hebrew Bible as God's punishment for wrongs committed. Because Saul does not listen to the voice of God, the kingdom "is torn out" of his hand (1 Sam. 28f); because David arranges to have Uriah the Hittite murdered and takes the latter's wife Bathsheba to himself his house is visited by misfortune (2 Sam. 12,9-12); because King Hosea (731-722 BC) does "what was evil in the sight of the Lord" (2 Kings 17,2) and "...the people of Israel had sinned against the Lord" (17,7) God delivers his people up to the enemy; in 722 Samaria is conquered by the King of Assur, and the northern kingdom destroyed.

God repeatedly threatens with sanctions, and he carries out these threats when his people are unfaithful to him, at the same time promising long-service bonuses to those who hold to him: "...for I the Lord your God am a jealous God, visiting the iniquity of the fathers upon the children of the third and fourth generation of those who hate me, but showing steadfast love to thousands of those who love me and keep my commandments" (Ex. 20,5f).

This retaliation theory was later modified and relativized — especially when it was taken into account that the innocent were also not spared from suffering, and that the godless often prospered wonderfully. At any rate Jeremiah and Ezekiel categorically deny that God will hold liable all members of a family for the crimes of one member; "The soul that sins shall die. The son

17

shall not suffer for the iniquity of the father, nor the father suffer for the iniquity of the son; the righteousness of the righteous shall be upon himself, and the wickedness of the wicked shall be upon himself'' (Ezek. 18,20; compare Jer.31,29f). At about the same time, that is, during the Babylonian exile (586-538 BC) the idea of doing atonement for someone else emerged, based on the fact that an innocent person could suffer *voluntarily* for the sins of another, in order to soothe God's wrath (see Is. 53). But here it was also assumed (as in Jeremiah and Ezekiel) that God would demand a corresponding atonement for every infringement of his law.

Concerning *the point of suffering*, it was later recognized that this can sometimes serve as purification or as a test. But as for the *reason for suffering*, people gradually began to understand that this question was hidden in God's mystery itself, and was therefore impossible to answer.

However, people did not entirely abandon the theory of retaliation because of this insight. They did, however, begin to comprehend that not every suffering represented a punishment from God. But as before, they were convinced that no sinner could escape from just punishment imposed by God.

At the time of Jesus this form of the retaliation theory was widely spread. Every human effort was inevitably followed by God's counter effort; every human action caused a divine reaction, corresponding to the principle of poetic justice. This meant that God could only be good to the good, and only good to sinners when they repented, and further, when they had done a penance that corresponded in severity to their guilt.

God cares, He does not punish

The thought of retaliation — or rather the thought of penance being done as a *condition* of forgiveness — is so convincing because it developed together with the idea of justice. So long as one applies this theory to the relationship between God and man, it can appear conclusive for the moment. But one first realizes just how problematic it is in reality, when one tries to transfer it to relationships between people.

Here is a man who has deceived his wife; he himself doesn't know why — the flesh was willing and the spirit weak... And now, having come to his senses again, this false step distresses him, and he regrets it from the bottom of his heart. But will his wife, who clings to him with all her being, reject him when he begs for forgiveness? Will she impose conditions on him before she even considers forgiving him?

Or there is a daughter, much loved by her parents. If she embezzles a couple of hundred dollars from her place of work, for some reason or another, and then sees her mistake, will her parents then say to her: "after a year has passed you may come home again, but during this time you must prove yourself. You must understand that we do need some evidence that you really mean to improve as you have promised." Isn't it far more likely that both the deceived wife and the disappointed parents, however much they have suffered, will be happy that they have reconciled, and that they determine never to hurt one another again?

This sort of experience from the area of human relationships may have led Jesus to ask the question how God might well react if a sinner should recognize his guilt, repent, and not shirk the consequences? The result of his reflection is a parable that many people consider to be his most beautiful story.

"There was a man who had two sons; and the younger of them said to his father, 'Father, give me the share of property that falls to me.' And he divided his living between them. Not many days later, the younger son gathered all he had, and took his journey into a far country, and there he squandered his property in loose living. And when he had spent everything, a great famine arose in that country, and he began to be in want. So he went and joined himself to one of the citizens of that country who sent him into his fields to feed swine. And he would gladly have fed on the pods that the swine ate; and no one gave him anything. But when he came to himself he said, 'How many of my father's hired servants have bread enough and to spare, but I perish here with hunger! I will arise and go to my father, and I will say to him 'Father, I have sinned against heaven and before you; I am no longer worthy to be called your son; treat me as one of your hired servants.' And he arose and came to his father. (Lk. 15,11-20)

What caused the son to set out or even more, to break out? Why does he want to get away at any price, although he obviously lacks nothing?

In his novel "The Diary of Malte Laurids Brigge" Rainer Maria Rilke expresses the conviction that "the story of the prodigal son is the legend of one who does not wish to be loved." The son feels so oppressed by the love that is shown to him on all sides that he doesn't even want the dogs around him because they too "have sympathy and concern in their eyes."[1] This supposition has something attractive about it, and yet at the same time the disadvantage that one finds no evidence whatsoever for it in the text. The development of the story seems rather to hint that the son experiences the ties to his family home as shackles, that he has had enough of getting good advice dished out to him with every plate of soup; that he longs for what is known as "life." He wants to taste freedom, and shape his existence according to his own ideas.

Obviously the father knows that the insights of experience cannot be passed on, in contrast to knowledge that can be learnt. At any rate he does not give us the impression that he wishes to restrain his son. He hands over his inheritance — the law at the time recognized that one could declare a last will and testament and transfer property at any time during one's life. The son goes into "a distant land" as if he could not put enough space between himself and his kin. He lives entirely according to his ideas — and something occurs that he has not imagined: in a short time he goes completely to the dogs, or, as the text says, he ends up at the pigs' trough. Two things are hinted at here, namely that the son is living in a pagan country, and that he can fall no further. It is well known that according to the Jews the pig is an unclean animal (Lev. 11,7), and this is the reason why the Talmud expressly curses pig breeders (Baba Qamma, 82b).

When the son has fallen as far as he can, he determines to change his ways. Hundreds of times in his thoughts he repeats the words that he will say to his father on his return. One day he stands before the house that he once belonged to, and in which now nothing more belongs to him.

"I have returned, I have crossed the fields, and look around me. It is my father's old farmyard. The puddle in the middle. Old, useless farm implements, muddled up together, block the way to the attic stairs. The cat lowers on the banisters. A torn cloth, once wound

around a pole in play, flutters in the wind. I have arrived. Who will receive me? Who waits behind the kitchen door? Smoke comes from the chimney, coffee is being made for the evening meal. Do you feel ill at ease, do you feel at home? I don't know, I feel very unsure. It is my father's house, but things stand coldly next to each other, as if each one is occupied with its own affairs, that I have partly forgotten and partly never knew. What use am I to them, what am I to them, even if I am the son of my father, the old landowner's son. And I do not dare to knock on the kitchen door, I only listen from a distance, standing so that I cannot be surprised as an eavesdropper. And while I listen from a distance, I hear nothing, I only hear the soft chime of a clock, or perhaps imagine that I have heard it from the days of childhood. Whatever else happens in the kitchen is the secret of those sitting there, which they keep from me. The longer one hesitates before the door, the stranger one becomes. How would it be if someone were now to open the door and ask me something? Would I then not myself be someone who wants to keep his secret?"

This monologue of the son comes from a sketch by Kafka. Max Brod, a friend and the editor of his most important works gave it the misleading title "Homecoming."[2]

At best it is about a return. "I have returned; I have arrived" maintains the "I" narrator. And to the question "do you feel ill at ease, do you feel at home?" he dares not reply. The smoke pouring from the chimney shows that someone is in the kitchen. But that does not mean that one remembers one's own kin. The familiar striking of the clock chiming as if "from childhood days" reminds him of earlier times. But the house in which he now finds himself again is no longer his home.

22

One is at home where someone is there waiting for one.

However this is not the point in Kafka. The man who has come back remains standing outside in front of the closed door. The text ends with this, and so one has the impression that the author himself might have been afraid that the father might turn his son away. The end of the story remains completely open. For this reason it has something uncannily oppressive about it.

On the other hand, Jesus tells his parable to the end. And at exactly the point where Kafka breaks off, there is a change of perspective in the narrative. What now happens is no longer seen from the son's point of view but from the father's.

"And he arose and came to his father. But while he was yet at a distance, his father saw him and had compassion, and ran and embraced him and kissed him. And the son said to him 'Father I have sinned against heaven and before you. I am no longer worthy to be called your son.' But the father said to his servants 'Bring quickly the best robe, and put it on him; and put a ring on his hand and shoes on his feet; and bring the fatted calf and kill it, and let us eat and make merry; for this my son was dead and is alive again; he was lost, and is found.' And they begun to make merry." (Lk. 15,20-24)

The fact that the father is keeping a lookout for his son, that he expects him and hurries towards him and arranges a joyful feast shows just how much his erring son still means to him: everything. Even those amongst Jesus's fellow countrymen who didn't have sharp ears at all immediately understood that he was illustrating God's behavior towards sinners in this story; and this is exactly what the parable amounts to. Also one must not overlook the fact that the father, although nothing is closer to his heart than the well-being of his son, initially does not make the slightest attempt to hold him back, intimating and in fact knowing (after all, he knows him very well) that his departure would be the beginning of disaster.

This father obviously differs from those parents who supposedly only "want the best" for their children, and interfere with their development precisely for this reason. They force them to aim at a career in which they themselves have failed for one reason or another. Or they press them to break off a relationship with a partner because this is not "befitting to their station." It goes without saying that parents always know best which bridegroom will make their daughter happy ever after! And certainly not all sons and daughters possess the necessary energy to stand up to them and — this is the point — "hurt them." Of those that do manage to take their lives into their own hands, many have guilt complexes for years, because, amongst other things, their parents let them feel their acute disappointment. If something should indeed misfire, then of course it is entirely due to the fact that the children did not want and did not do what their parents had planned for them, these parents who only meant well. Meant well for whom?

We may assume that the father in Jesus's parable also brought up both his sons most carefully. Now they are grown up. The story allows us to conclude that the youngest son is still unmarried; he must be between seventeen and twenty-two, if one takes the social customs of the time into account; at an age when one must make up one's own mind about the values one is to choose. The father knows that one cannot hold a young man back when he has got it into his head to live his own life. However much he may suffer for it, he gives

24

his son his freedom. Or more exactly, he releases him to freedom.

Freedom? Obviously the son understands this quite differently from his father; that is, to cast off his shackles, free himself from obligations, and have the chance to make up his own mind without having to let a natural authority make decisions for him as usual. Basically he is really looking for what he believes he cannot find at home: himself. As Jesus uses no word to imply that the son wants to end his relationship to his father, we also don't need to think up any base motive for him. The son does not intend to cause a break; he simply needs some distance. Although he believes he is a master of himself he has really long been a slave to his vices. He does what pleases him, and becomes the victim of his passions.

So Jesus's story about God's love also proves to be a lesson about freedom. The son seeks freedom, confusing it with caprice. During the course of a painful process of learning, he begins to understand that freedom does not consist in the absence of commitment; on the contrary, it is only possible within a particular form of commitment. It is only within his father's house that the son really possesses all the rights of a son. In foreign parts he is conditioned by the foreign; he gets caught up in ever newer dependencies. This commitment to the father (the implication, of course, is to God) is virtually imperative if a person is not to fall victim, as the son had done, to the second-rate — usually to some ideology, which then, irresponsibly, he makes into his idol. Only responsibility towards a decisive authority in the outer world can make a person free towards all that is the inner-world. Expressed religiously: in the face of social pressures, state laws and church regulations it is only by referring to his conscience — in which he hears the voice of God — that the believer can freely and safely say: Here I stand, I can no other.

A Gentle God

The son has to reach rock bottom before he realizes that absolute lack of commitment leads to absolute slavery, and why this is so. So obviously this parable also teaches us that first there is need of error and detour before anyone can find freedom and inner maturity. But Jesus does not content himself with this alone: his story is also concerned with the fact that one may not obstruct the way back for a person who has learned from his mistakes.

It is not that the father minimizes or condones his son's behavior. There are neither accomplice's winks ("It isn't so bad after all") nor companionable thumps on the back ("We're only human after all"). The son is quite aware that he has really done everything wrong that he could do. Because he sees this himself, his father does not have to refer to it; only one thing is left to him: to rejoice from a full heart.

This is the aim of the whole story. God cares for the one who has sought life's happiness in the wrong place like a mother who has one child sick among many, and is there for this child alone at this precise moment. Such a thought is so near to Jesus's heart that he also makes it the basis of two further stories.

"What man of you, having a hundred sheep, if he has lost one of them, does not leave the ninety-nine in the wilderness, and go after the one which is lost, until he finds it? And when he has found it, he lays it on his shoulders, rejoicing. And when he comes home, he calls together his friends, and his neighbors, saying to them 'Rejoice with me, for I have found my sheep which was

lost.' Just so, I tell you, there will be more joy in heaven over one sinner who repents than over ninety-nine righteous persons who need no repentance.

Or what woman, having ten silver coins, if she loses one coin, does not light a lamp and sweep the house and seek diligently until she finds it? And when she has found it, she calls together her friends and neighbors, saying 'Rejoice with me, for I have found the coin which I lost.' Just so, I tell you, there is joy among the angels of God over one sinner who repents." (Lk. 15,4-10; see Mt. 18,12-14).

The drachma is a coin of little worth; it would just about pay for a family's daily needs. But if you live from hand to mouth, it represents a considerable sum. We can therefore understand why the woman, as soon as she notices her loss, pulls open the door and lights a lamp in the windowless living room. She goes over the stone floor with a broom so that she can hear the clink of the coin in the half darkness.

The behavior of the shepherd is more puzzling. He leaves his whole flock alone in order to go after one lost sheep. May we assume that he trusts the other animals to the care of another shepherd? Perhaps. But the very fact that there is no mention of this shows us what the story is about; simply and solely seeking and finding. And of course about the boundless joy there is in heaven when one sinner comes home to God.

All these three stories together represent a unity within Luke's gospel that in the end concerns the image of God. The God that Jesus proclaims is also attached to sinners with a boundless love.

If Jesus says that there is more joy in heaven over one sinner willing to repent than over ninety-nine righteous persons, we can expect that the people of his world themselves rejoiced over the good news. But it seems that there was not unqualified agreement on earth about some of the things that were determined in heaven.

Jesus brings this bitter experience into his parable of the prodigal son. We have reserved the conclusion for now.

"Now his elder son was in the field; and as he came and drew near to the house, he heard music and dancing. And he called one of the servants and asked what this meant. And he said to him 'Your brother has come, and your father has killed the fatted calf, because he has received him safe and sound.' But he was angry and refused to go in. His father came out and entreated him, but he answered his father 'Lo, these many years I have served you, and I never disobeyed your command; yet you never gave me a kid, that I might make merry with my friends. But when this son of yours came, who has devoured your living with harlots, you killed for him the fatted calf!' And he said to him 'Son, you are always with me, and all that is mine is yours. It was fitting to make merry and be glad, for this your brother was dead, and is alive; he was lost, and is found.'" (Lk. 15,25-32).

This final scene is the answer to those who found Jesus's mixing with tax collectors and sinners offensive. The assumption that God would first turn towards a sinner when he had repented and done penance was widespread. As long as this did not happen, the sinner remained outside the circle of the pious; he was only acceptable to society when he had paid off his fault. For this reason the elder son cannot understand at all that his father should arrange a feast as soon as his brother returns. How come? No penance? No word of expia-

28

tion? Not the slightest hint of satisfaction? That was indeed too much of a good thing.

Here one sees the remarkable originality of Jesus's message although there may have been many fellow Jews who thought like this. We know of scripture commentaries from the first century of our calendar (which goes back over a long tradition) that tend towards the same direction. For example one Midrash says "Repentance and remorse are common to all sacrifices"[3] and this can only mean that God has already forgiven a sinner at the moment of his guilt, when he has gained insight and decides to repent. However, this thought does not seem to have been widespread in post-biblical Judaism. At any rate the gospels in their entirety document the fact that a majority of Jesus's contemporaries vehemently defended the "traditional" teaching of justification. Of course, the representatives of this view did not exclude the idea that God could grant forgiveness to a sinner. Nevertheless we are not just concerned with the possibility of forgiveness here, but with the conditions usually attached to it. Only after a sinner had seriously put his will to repent to the test through good works, fasting, prayer, and patience in enduring suffering, and thereby proved his worth, might he hope to achieve God's favor.

In this respect Jesus represented another point of view, and in order to proclaim its credibility, he had to turn towards those who were moral failures; how else could he make them understand that their names too were written on the heart of God? In doing this he simply stood the prevalent teaching of justification on its head. Jesus taught that God did not need any previous demonstration of good will in the form of proving one's worth in order to forgive a sinner. As the return of the prodigal son is enough for the father, so the repentance of the sinner is enough for God. Not only does God not attach any conditions to his turning towards his people; he is actually consumed with anxiety for them.

That Jesus justified his parables of the shepherd and the lost sheep, the housewife and the lost drachma, and the merciful father to those who were offended by his behavior towards sinners emerges from the evangelist's introductory remark: "now the tax collectors and sinners were all drawing near to hear him. And the Pharisees and the scribes murmured saying, 'This man receives sinners and eats with them'" (Lk. 15,1-2; see Mt. 9,10-13). The following transition "so he told them this parable" (Lk. 15,3) aims at showing that Jesus's behavior reflects God's attitude towards those who feel themselves to be lost. Certainly these stories deal first with the teaching on justification and thus with the question as to how the guilty person can be justified before God. But at the same time they are always concerned with the image of God as well.

This is particularly marked in the parable of the prodigal son. Although Israel had depicted God very early on as Father: "Thou O Lord, art our Father, our Redeemer from of old is thy name" (Is. 63,16; see 64,7; see Tob. 13,4), it is perhaps less known that God's image at that time also showed maternal features. So the strong "arm of the Lord" is occasionally felt as the gentle hand of a woman: "as one whom his mother comforts, so will I comfort you" (Is. 66,13; see 49,15; Hos. 11,1-4). Admittedly these womanly and maternal features of God were covered up by a strict father image. At any rate, both the sons in the parable of the prodigal son seem to have been caught up in the concept of an authoritarian father. The younger is only able to correct this after his unsuccessful experiment. His brother tends towards the same prejudice. He complains that his father has never even given him a kid, although he has always served him faithfully and devotedly. This reproach is revealing. The elder son fixes all his attention on manners — or more precisely — on commandments and regulations, which he then naturally finds a burden. His descendants are those Christians whose whole lives of faith amount to a kind of religious competitive sport because they overlook the fact that God's directives simply serve the good of mankind. Observed more closely, their so-called love of God proves to be a highly ambivalent attitude, in which the desire for reward and the fear of punishment are equally balanced. From the beginning misunderstandings of this kind cannot be ruled out in the Jewish conception of God the father.

"Our Father": in Hebrew the word is *abbinu* which has a very ceremonious, reverential, and above all authoritative ring to it. Yet when Jesus turns to the father and invites his own to do the same, he does not use *abbinu,* but the form of address used in his Aramaic mother-tongue, which is *abba*; dear, good Dad.

It is the daily, trustingly familiar way of addressing the father which comes from childhood speech. Devotion and trust, warmth and respect, love, gratitude, attachment, and above all tenderness and gentleness are all contained in the word *abba.* It is of *this* God that Jesus speaks over and over again in his parables, and it is a fact that people who eke out their existences far away from God's wisdom and promises are the most likely to understand what Jesus wants to say in his stories: God does not exclude one single person from his company; he does not nail anyone to his past; and he receives with open arms those who turn to him. Like the whiteness of new snow covering the earth, God's

31

mercy lies upon every human being who searches for him with the whole longing of his heart.

2

God Knows No Love
that can be Bought

*"Gregory Samsa woke from uneasy dreams one
morning to find himself changed into a giant bug. He
was lying on his back, which was of a shell-like hard-
ness, and when he lifted his head a little he could see
his dome-shaped brown belly, banded with what looked
like reinforcing arches, on top of which his quilt, while
threatening to slip off completely at any moment, still
maintained a precarious hold. His many legs, pitifully
thin in relation to the rest of him, threshed ineffectually
before his eyes."*[1]

Gregory and his seventeen year old sister live with
their parents. After the collapse of his father's business,
he takes a job as a commercial traveller, and provides
for the family. Of course, on this particular morning,
he does not manage to get to work on time. Gradually
it becomes clear to him that he will have to give up his
work completely, and that the members of his family
will soon start reacting to his inexplicable state with
horror and disgust, and then with despair and fear.

When Gregory realizes what repugnance he causes,
he hides himself away for days under the sofa in his
bedroom. His sister, who formerly showed great affection for him, sometimes puts some pieces of garbage or
the remnants of meals out for him. But when he begins
to creep up the walls, she too begins to fear him, and

behaves with increasing coldness and hostility towards him. One day, as he ventures into the living room through the door left open by chance, and releases real panic among the family just through his mere presence, his father decides to "bombard" him with apples. One of them sinks into his back and remains "lodged in his flesh as a visible reminder." Even his sister now considers how they "can get rid of this creature."

One evening the door of the living room is again left open, and Gregory creeps in, attracted by his sister's violin playing. His parents and three tenants who have just moved in and are unaware of his existence are collected there. They react to the sight of him with such horror that Gregory flees back to his room in panic.

"The rotten apple in his back and the inflamed area around it, now completely covered with a soft dust, were almost forgotten. He recalled his family with sympathy and love. His own belief that he must go was if possible even firmer than his sister's. He remained in this state of vacant and peaceable reflection until the church clock struck three in the morning. He lived to see the first signs of the general brightening outside the window. Then independently of his will, his head sank to the floor and his last breath streamed feebly from his nostrils."

"...that you would stamp me down"

Understandably this strange story (Franz Kafka's tale "The Metamorphosis") has experienced diverse and often contradictory interpretations. To me the crucial question is, how does a writer come to such a subject, and what causes him to develop it into a story? There is an answer to this in the famous "Letter to my Father" which Kafka wrote at the age of 36 in 1919. The beginning of this shows us that it is not only a report about the writer's relationship to his father, but at the same time a kind of reckoning.

"Dear Father, you asked me once quite recently, why I maintain that I was afraid of you. As usual, I did not know how to answer you, partly out of this fear I have of you, and partly because too many details are attached to the basis of it for me to be able to bring them even roughly together in speech"[2] . .

This fear is deeply rooted; it goes back to childhood years.

"I was already depressed by your mere physical presence. For example, I remember how we used to undress together in a (bathing) cabin. I, thin, weak, pigeon shouldered; you, strong, tall, broad shouldered. Even then in the cabin I felt I was pitiful, not only before you, but before the whole world, because you were the measure of all things to me. Then we stepped out of the cabin in front of all the people, I holding your hand, a little skeleton, unsure, bare-footed on the planks, afraid of the water, incapable of imitating the swimming movements that you constantly made in front of me. You made them with good intentions towards me, but in fact they were a great shame to me because I was in deep despair, and at such moments all the bad experiences in all areas of my life harmonized magnificently together."

From a purely theoretical point of view, the opposite reactions are also thinkable; the child could experience the father's power and strength as protective, not as terrifying. On the other hand, the fact that on the purely physical level the child sees the father only as a threatening super power and not at all as a protector, has grounds conditioned by experience. He sees his father as an authority that can no longer be analyzed, as the final authority. In other words, all that the father thinks, all that he says, all that he does, has somehow a divine character.

"You ruled the world from your armchair. Your view was right, every one else was mad, hysterical, meshuga, not normal. At the same time your self-confidence was so great that you didn't have to be at all consequential, yet you did not stop being right. It could also happen that you had no opinion at all about something, and consequently all other possible opinions on the subject had to be wrong without exception. For example, you could complain about the Czechs, then the Germans, then about the Jews, not only indiscriminately, but in every respect, until finally there was no one left apart from you. You became something mysterious for me, a quality possessed by all tyrants, whose rights are based upon their person, and not on their thoughts. At least it seemed so to me. One was absolutely defenseless before you."

Having this background in mind, we can now appreciate that in his story "The Metamorphosis" Kafka is not depicting an imaginary horror scene almost bordering on the perverse, but putting his own horrendous experiences into a code. This observation is not dependent on mere assumption, but verified by the shocking letter in which the son holds out his hands towards his father: "My letters are about you, I only lament in them what I could not lament upon your breast."

In his letter Kafka reminds his father that he always rejected from the start anything that was at all important to the son; "that applied to my thoughts as well as to people (I was friendly with"). His father described the latter without further ado as "dogs and fleas" and as "pests"(!). Naturally this kind of debasement leaves traces because the father is "such an atrocious author-ity" from whom the son can only "creep" into his room.

This letter that Kafka actually never sent -—because he was afraid? -—is the most important key to deci-phering the hieroglyphics in which "The Metamorpho-sis" is written.

Gregory Samsa turns into a pest overnight because he has long felt himself to be one. When he not only creeps back into his room but also hides under the sofa he does this out of pure fear of his father's stamping feet and swinging stick. He is divided from his father not only by a closed door but by worlds. Because this almighty father can never be wrong under any circumstances, Gregory is convinced that all other people (mother, sister, the lodgers, the maid) see a "monster" in him, and therefore he must spare them his presence. We know that Gregory dies from the fatal wound that his father inflicted upon him when he threw the apples at him. Here the novelist puts into code what the letter writer expresses clearly, that "one could have accepted that you would simply stamp me down, so that nothing more remained of me."

Of course Kafka's father did not destroy his son physically; and as far as the psychological damage is concerned, Kafka firmly maintains right at the begin-ning of his letter that he is concerned with a description of his feelings and not with a moral allocation of guilt.

"By which I constantly request you not to forget that I have never remotely believed in any guilt on your side. You act on me as you must act, but you should stop holding it as a particular wickedness on my part, that I am the victim of your acting upon me."

Kafka literally feels himself crushed by his father, and this does not change when he begins to succeed as a writer; on the contrary. When he gives his father his newest book, the latter's sole reaction to this challenge is to put it on his night table. The father has other expectations for his son, and because the son knows that he cannot fulfill them, he feels himself small and miserable in front of "this atrociously authoritative person." In short, one cannot love such a person because one is afraid of him. And because one cannot do anything right in his eyes, the mere thought of him conjures up feelings of guilt.

Devotion without Payment in Advance

Doubtless many people are more fortunate in their fathers, and yet the mechanism here described is only too familiar to them. They experience a similar tragedy in their dealings with their God.

God appears as an overpowerful and therefore overwhelming authority, who inevitably reacts by withdrawing love if one does not fulfill all expectations. As these expectations frequently overreach human powers, one can never quite meet them. The result is a feeling of guilt which interacts with the expectations of earthly authorities and is unwilling to change.

One only needs to transfer the father-son relationship analyzed by Kafka to the religious level in order to grasp what is often played out between God and man — and the spiritual breakdown this can lead to.

"Gigantic in every way" was Kafka's experience of his father, who was of course above all the commandments he laid down for his son.

"Thus the world was divided into three parts for me. There was one where I lived as a slave under laws that

*were laid down only for me, and which, what is more,
I could never completely come up to, I don't know why.
Then there was a second world, infinitely far distant
from mine, where you lived, busy with governing, with
sending out commands, and with the annoyance caused
by no one following them. Finally there was a third
world, where all the other people lived, happily and free
from commands and obedience. I was constantly in
disgrace; either I followed your orders, and that was a
disgrace because they were only valid for me; or I was
defiant and that was also a disgrace, for how dared I
be defiant with you; or I couldn't follow because I didn't
have your strength, for example, your appetite, or your
skill, although you demanded these of me as self-evident; and this was the greatest disgrace. In this way the
child's reflection was not touched, only its feeling."*

Even when reason tells you that you know better,
you always have the feeling that everything you do is
wrong, you fail, you are a total bungler. "From all
sides I was in your debt" Kafka complains in another
part of the letter. One can only intimate how vast these
feelings of guilt must be if the person affected by them
feels himself a "monster" and "vermin."

This is found in the religious area precisely where
people sense themselves to be the opposite, or — more
accurately — subordinate to a God who is only waiting
to "stamp them down," giving them the impression that
they are living "in shame." The pressure to do well that
believers in *this* God suffer from can sometimes extend
to physical illness. Even the bare thought of having
failed in some way or another creates fear because they
must accept that God has disowned them for this reason.
It is not the failure as such which is so terrible, but
rather the idea that God's love has been forfeited

because of it. Eugen Drewermann has shown to what this kind of fear eventually leads.

"I understand very well that people who are afraid and are left alone in their fear can only have the feeling that they must force something total, something perfect, something absolute out of themselves — in fact something God-like. They may not make any more mistakes, may not fail, may not do anything that could be criticized, or anything that might set them apart. They must be like a ball, rolled up within itself; with no need to amend, no need of an opposite partner; in fact no more need of love. The tragedy is that this state only prolongs fear, and finally establishes the logic of fear; in the end hurling them into a world that no longer recognizes pity, but only judgment, hiding away, concealment, condemnation."[3]

This leads to man being no longer able to live his faith freely and with conviction. He mechanically fulfills a quota of religious obligations out of pure fear, is relieved when his quota is reached and yet he is never really happy in life. It is therefore easy to understand that if man's relationship to God is confined to mere feelings of duty, there can be no question of *human* relationship. Man's limitations can so overpower him that he is only able to experience shame and despair over his failings.

On the other hand he can try to receive God's directives seriously as objectives, and take them to heart. For it is only the liberating admission of one's own need for help that can protect one from a fatal attempt at self-redemption. Only those who have learned to accept all their mistakes and inadequacies are able to speak to God from a full heart; look at my empty hands; I am not able to realize the true good alone; only if you come towards me can I come a little nearer to you, and so find the way to myself at the same time.

The inability to step before God entirely naked, as it were, is of course part of our daily experiences. We all know that others approach us with reserve if we do not come up to their expectations, or even punish us with "withdrawal of love." The worst of all fears is the fear of not being loved. More or less unconsciously we so often try to buy the sympathy of another by conforming to his expectations. As a rule we don't take into account that efforts of this nature rest upon an illusion. As long as a person is accepted only because of particular characteristics or ways of behavior, devotion towards him is devotion to a thing, and not to a person. Now transfer this type of relationship mechanism between people to the religious plane, (and that is so self-explanatory that it hardly needs reflecting on), and from the angle of pure feeling you will think that you have to "represent" something before God, too, so that he will at least honor you with a look.

It is precisely this opinion that Jesus rejects so uncompromisingly. God does not make his devotion to people dependent upon a religious advance payment. He takes them as they are. This is expressed in a most provocative way in one of the parables.

"For the kingdom of heaven is like a householder who went out early in the morning to hire laborers for his vineyard. After agreeing with the laborers for a denarius a day, he sent them into his vineyard. And going out about the third hour he saw others standing idle in the market place; and to them he said 'You go into the vineyard too, and whatever is right I will give you.' So they went. Going out again about the sixth hour and the ninth hour, he did the same. And about the eleventh hour he went out and found others standing; and he said

to them 'Why do you stand here idle all day?' They said to him 'Because no one has hired us.' He said to them 'You go into the vineyard too.' And when evening came and the owner of the vineyard said to his steward 'Call the laborers and pay them their wages, beginning with the last, up to the first.' And when those hired about the eleventh hour came, each of them received a denarius. Now when the first came, they thought they would receive more; but each of them also received a denarius. And receiving it they grumbled at the householder, saying 'These last worked only one hour, and yet you have made them equal to us who have borne the burden of the day and the scorching heat.' But he replied to one of them 'Friend, I am doing you no wrong; did you not agree with me for a denarius? Take what belongs to you, and go; I choose to give this to the last as I give to you. Am I not allowed to do what I choose with what belongs to me? Or do you begrudge my generosity?' So the last will be first, and the first last." (Mt. 20,1-16).

Even the church fathers interpreted this parable in quite different ways. For example, Bishop Irenaeus of Lyon who suffered a martyr's death in 202 saw five periods of time in the Jewish-Christian history of salvation symbolized in the householder's five invitations. On the other hand, the Greek church scholar Origen, one of the most significant theologians of early Christianity who died c. 254 probably in Tyros (today Sur in Lebanon), equated the number five with the various ages of life during which people are converted to Christianity.

However, this kind of symbolic interpretation bypasses the message in the parable; the point is not that all the workers, apart from the length of their hours of work, finally get *their* wage, but that all of them get *the same* wage. This fact, which astonished both the characters in the parable and those listening to it, is of supreme significance in the understanding of the story.

In order to clear the path to the heart of the message, we must first of all explain a couple of inconsistencies. We are surprised that the owner of the vineyard had first to hire his workers. But due to the widespread unemployment at that time, the majority of the population had no chance of getting secure employment, and were forced to keep themselves alive on day wages. Normally landowners or their stewards would have looked for the work force they needed in the early morning at the market place, which was also a kind of job center. It would have been most unusual for a vineyard owner to have recruited work forces at three hourly intervals to start with, and then once again at the eleventh hour, that is, the late afternoon at five o'clock. There could be a number of reasons; for example, he may have taken into account that time was advancing, or that the work of the men he had already engaged did not come up to his expectations, or that the weather threatened to change. But as there are no definite comments along these lines, it seems pointless to speculate. Most probably this rather unusual detail is simply made necessary by the teaching Jesus wants to convey in this story. This is also true of the fact that the workers hired first are paid last, otherwise they would not have heard that all of them were going to receive the same wage. We may also assume that those who came last were almost as astonished as they were delighted by their preferential treatment.

Certainly most of the listeners at the time would have identified themselves entirely with the indignant workers who had been hired first. They only put into words what the listeners had on the tips of their tongues; that it was unjust, simply outrageous, to pay a whole day's wage to those workers who had only worked for a bare hour when the heat of the day had passed.

The employer finds this objection a totally unnecessary meddling in his affairs. He reminds the protestors that they had all agreed to a day's wage of a denarius. That was the normal rate at the time, and corresponded to the minimum living wage.

In our understanding of this story, it is important that we realize that this indeed unusual behavior of the vineyard owner did not spring from an arbitrary or high handed attitude or simply from a momentarily generous mood. He declares that he has acted deliberately, that is, out of pure goodness. At the same time he expresses the fear that those who feel that they have been swindled do not rebel for reasons of justice, but out of pure envy; "Do you begrudge my generosity?"

We do not discover whether the householder sticks to his opinion, or whether he allows himself to be convinced. It is not important to know this. What is far more essential is that Matthew passes on the question Jesus asks his readers -—- and asks us! And that we find the right answer.

Obviously Jesus is defending his own behavior in this story; he rebukes those who object to his mixing with people who are considered rejected by God. It is to these people that Jesus turns, at the same time giving us to understand that God's love for them is no less than for those who toil in precise observation of the law. In other words, Jesus draws a picture of God that appeared so utterly strange to his fellow countrymen that it must have seemed like a caricature to them.

Just how controversial this parable of the generous householder in fact was, can best be understood if we compare it to a rabbinical story, which, in spite of many similarities, contains a diametrically opposed teaching.

"A King engaged a great number of workers. Two hours after they had begun their work, he visited them. He saw that one of them stood out from all the rest by reason of his diligence and skill. He took him by the hand, and strolled up and down with him until evening. When the workers came to receive their wages, each one received the same sum as all the others. Then they grumbled among themselves and said: 'We have worked all day, and this man has only done two hours, and in spite of this you have paid him the same wage!' But the King replied 'I do you no injustice by this; this worker did more in two hours than you in a whole day.'"[A]

It is likely that the rabbi credited with this story by the Talmud did not know that in all probability it went back to the parable of the vineyard owner. This later story has been so re-modelled that its original sense has been turned around completely, and it has been re-harmonized into the generally accepted Jewish image of God. The one worker who toils for only two hours receives the same pay as the others because he has achieved the same results in a shorter time. This corresponds exactly to Jewish thinking of the time. God gives each person the wages that he *merits*. This view is grounded in the Jewish teaching of justification, or more exactly, in the early Jewish understanding of the Torah.[5] According to this, Israel's directive was given exclusively for the purpose of earning merits by obedience to it. These merits in their turn are followed by God's wages. The greater the merits a person can show, logically the richer the reward he is entitled to. When belief in life after death became more common in Judaism at about the middle of the 2nd century BC, people began to reckon with the possibility that God —

weighing both justice and guilt — would pay out this reward if need be in the next world.

Among the broad mass of people this thinking led mainly to the obsession with reward as the principal motive for ethical dealing. An example of this is the story passed down by the Talmud of a widow who regularly looked for a synagogue quite some distance away although she lived in the immediate neighborhood of one. When Rabbi Joachanan (he died in 279) asked her for an explanation, she replied with astonishment "Rabbi, shan't I be rewarded for my walk?" Taking the long way was considered a greater service before God. Rabbi Joachanan, one of the most celebrated teachers of his time, thought this woman's behavior should be emulated.[6]

On the other hand, according to the witness of the Talmud, there were many pious individuals who fought against this sort of petty mindedness; we are reminded of the warning of Antigonos of Socho, who probably lived about 180 BC: "Do not be like stewards who serve their master on condition they receive rewards, but be like stewards who serve their master without condition, and the fear of heaven be on you!"[7] The belief that in the end it was not achievement but basic convictions that counted was not entirely unknown in Judaism: "It's all the same, whether one does a lot or a little, as long as one turns one's heart towards God." But then such voices, differing from the generally accepted teaching on reward, are the exceptions. They did not seem to get through to the ordinary people.

Jesus had seized upon a thought which was not foreign to at least some of his contemporaries, but which had not been put into general practice.

One could of course raise the objection that Jesus too seemed sometimes to employ this way of thinking about reward. Although the individual day workers produce different amounts of work, the dinarius they receive is nevertheless the reward for it. Does that perhaps mean that God's devotion and goodness are indeed conditioned by the special services of men?

In fact a discussion about the question of reward takes place among the disciples immediately before he tells the parable; they want to know what those who follow Jesus can expect (see Mt. 19, 27-30). The answer is that they are to "receive a hundred fold and inherit eternal life" (19. 29); infinitely more than they could ever earn! In other words, God's "reward" is in every case a gift so large that one can never earn it by work. To express this once more in a different way: the "reward" here spoken about (and afterwards in the parable of the generous employer which follows later) is — and only another paradox can help us — a pure *reward of mercy*, the debt-free gift of an eternally good God.

Against Yes-Men and Smooth Talkers

The short parable about the father and his two sons that one could also describe as the story of the yes-man and the no-man aims in the same direction. Again it is about working in a vineyard, and again there is a polemic highpoint.

"...A man had two sons; and he went to the first and said 'Son, go and work in the vineyard today.' And he answered, 'I will not;' but afterward he repented and went. And he went to the second, and said the same; and he answered 'I go sir,' but did not go. Which of the two did the will of his father?" (Mt. 21. 28-31).

The final question is obviously purely rhetorical. At first it seems as if Jesus is proceeding from a somewhat

47

simple alternative — to put it mildly. This alternative is sometimes brought forward amongst Christians today by those who distance themselves from parish life, justifying this by saying that people who constantly run to church are certainly no better for it, and that the not so pious are generally much more pleasant. Heinrich Böll's famous clown formulates this rather more aptly: "The children of the world are more warm-hearted than the children of light."[8]

In view of the clown's personal situation — a church functionary has made off with his girl friend — his statement is understandable. But Jesus's parable aims in an entirely different direction. By the yes-men he means those who clearly lay more worth on the teaching of faith than on the living of faith. But he in no way maintains that all pious people are hypocrites who forget their duty. We are not debating this platitude. This short and yet pregnant parable is much more concerned with the balance of importance: what use is it to pray piously if one is also not ready to knuckle down cheerfully? What is all this wringing of hands in the temple about, if one does not open one's arms for fellow human beings? (Compare Hos. 6,6 to Mt. 9,13; 12,7). How fruitful is it to praise God with one's lips if one's heart is far from him? (Compare Is. 29,13 to Mk 7,6). Basically Jesus seizes upon an idea here that had already been expressed a generation earlier by Rabbi Schammai: "Make it a firm rule that the instructions are understood. But speak little and do much!"[9]

Jesus relates his story of the two sons particularly to those who are convinced that they "do much," namely to "the chief priests and the elders of the people" (Mt.21,23). He is obviously reproaching them because in their doings they basically miss the point. This becomes clear if we draw upon Jesus's other words to groups of influential persons to help us interpret the parable. These groups go way beyond Mosaic Law — which merely allows for the tenfold increase of the fruits of the field, of corn, wine and oil (Dtn. 14,22f) — even to extending it to kitchen herbs, mint, dill, cumin, while neglecting "the weightier matters of the law, justice and mercy and faith" (Mt. 23,23). Basically they are no more than yes-men and smooth talkers, who brag about their petty minded little doings, and in reality overlook what is decisive.

Jesus faces these people with the "no men," not however meaning those who admittedly could not care less about the whole profession of faith, but do care about their fellow human beings. He does not mean the non-believers or those who have other beliefs, but the sinners, willing to repent and free from any exaggerated self-evaluation, who think of converting their change of mind into deeds. It is these people that he contrasts with the "yes-men." There is no doubt about this in the following words of Jesus:

"Truly I say to you, (the chief priests and the elders of the people) the tax collectors and the harlots go into the kingdom of God before you. For John came to you in the way of righteousness, and you did not believe him, but the tax collectors and the harlots believed him; and even when you saw it, you did not afterward repent and believe him" (Mt, 21,31f).

In this Jesus contrasts the religious leaders he speaks to in the parable — who have not gone "the way of righteousness" — with the tax collectors and harlots, who have changed their minds or are even determined to repent. In other words, their previous "No" — and that means the whole of their earlier lives — does not prevent God from taking them into the community of his kingdom.

49

The parable of the father and the two sons, therefore, contains in shortened form the whole of Jesus's good tidings, which are tantamount to saying that the sincere will to reform is enough to bring man to salvation, and that he can accept this salvation gladly and thankfully from God's hand.

It was probably Matthew who first coupled Jesus's words of the tax collectors' and sinners' pre-eminence with the parable of the two sons. Luke also knew about this tradition, but in him we find it in a somewhat different connection. Jesus commissions the messengers of John, who is in prison, to tell him of his works. Afterwards he himself speaks about the Baptist.

"When they heard this all the people and the tax collectors justified God, having been baptized with the baptism of John; but the Pharisees and lawyers rejected the purpose of God for themselves, not having been baptized by him." (Lk. 7,29f).

What it all depends on

In another example Jesus himself also illustrates the words that Matthew has employed in the parable of the two sons.

"He also told this parable to some who trusted in themselves that they were righteous and despised others: 'Two men went up into the temple to pray, one a Pharisee and the other a tax collector. The Pharisee stood and prayed thus with himself, 'God, I thank thee that I am not like other men, extortioners, unjust, adulterers, or even like this tax collector. I fast twice a week, I give tithes of all that I get.' But the tax collector, standing far off, would not even lift up his eyes to heaven, but beat his breast, saying, 'God be merciful to me a sinner!' I tell you, this man went down to his

house justified rather than the other; for every one who exalts himself will be humbled, but he who humbles himself will be exalted.'" (Lk. 18,9-14).

This particular story has doubtless contributed to the Pharisees having a bad press among Christians even today. In reality of course, Jesus was initially very close to the Pharisees. In contrast to the party of the Sadducees whose members sprung from the priestly aristocracy, the Pharisees were recruited from the craftsmen of the middle classes, a group to which, because of his background, Jesus also belonged. The Pharisees formed a lay movement, and their religious leaders had a high reputation among the people. Their main concern was the strictest possible observance of the law. This led to their gradually distancing themselves from the lowest strata of society, already considered "unclean" because they often did not know the specific writings of the law, and therefore could not observe them.

The conflict between Jesus and the Pharisees did not have its origin in his disparagement of their teachings. Their daily behavior as an elite group ("the isolated ones," as their opponents described them) was a constant irritant — and not only in religious matters. The episode of the Sabbath feast in the house of a Pharisee, handed down by Luke, is characteristic of this. As Jesus noticed how the guests — obviously those learned in the scriptures, teachers of the law, and Pharisees — all rushed for the places of honor, he took this as an opportunity to tell them "a parable" (Lk. 14,7):

"When you are invited by anyone to a marriage feast, do not sit down in the place of honor, lest a more eminent man than you be invited by him; and he who invited you both will come and say to you 'Give place to this man' and then you will begin with shame to take

51

the lowest place. But when you are invited, go and sit in the lowest place, so that when your host comes he may say to you 'Friend, go up higher'; then you will be honored in the presence of all who sit at table with you. For every one who exalts himself will be humbled, and he who humbles himself will be exalted" (Lk. 14,8-11).

At that time — very much as today — places at table were not ordered according to preference of age, but according to the reputation of the guests. The guest also found himself a place commensurate with his position. The question of seating, particularly among the learned Jews, was not a minor matter, especially as they were accustomed to inferring order of rank from seating order.[10]

It is not by chance that Jesus ends his parable of the humble guest with the same warning as in the parable of the Pharisee and the tax collector.

Incidentally, the Pharisee who prays in the temple is not a caricature in any way; like most of his colleagues of the time he is strictly observant of the law. He makes an effort to fulfill the law in minutest detail. Jesus does not condemn this attitude at all. Instead he tacitly assumes that here we are talking about an example worthy of imitation. It is also not implied that the Pharisee stands up front so that other people can see him. He does not boast of his good works in a loud voice before the people. He thanks God in his thoughts, without moving his lips; "he prays to himself" might be a translation.

Yet in a sense we are talking about an "un-holy" prayer. Instead of fixing his gaze on God, his glance falls on a poor sinner who just happens to be there, and he creates a distinctive personal image for himself at this man's expense.

52

As we see from the great continuity — (compare Lk.17,22; 18,1;9; 19,11) — this parable belongs to the directives for the disciples. It is not against the Pharisees. Instead, the sharpest point is aimed at some of Jesus's sympathizers and disciples, "because they were righteous and despised others" (Lk. 18,9) — (Could they possibly have thought they were following Jesus here!) In short, in this story Jesus wants to warn his own followers of vain, misanthropic self-justification.

At the same time he justifies his own generous behavior towards tax collectors and sinners, knowing that many have reproached him for this.

According to (pharisaic) understanding at the time, the people regarded as sinners were not only those who led immoral lives, but also those who practiced a disreputable trade (e.g. grave diggers or tanners because their work brought them into contact with corpses, making them unclean), or those who practiced a profession tempting them to dishonesty (e.g.traders and particularly tax collectors). The latter leased their tax offices from Rome. Although the tariffs were set by the Roman authorities, they were handled in such a way by the tax collectors that a considerable profit remained after the rent had been deducted. For this reason they were hated by the populace. According to pharisaic understanding they were regarded as sinners because they cultivated contact with the heathen Romans, and according to general conviction, they were to be avoided if at all possible.

Naturally Jesus was aware of how offensive his story would be if he allowed a tax collector, of all people, to appear in it, but he then went on to explain in a way that could not be misunderstood that this man would be acceptable to God. In keeping with the current interpretation of the law, there was only one way open

53

to this tax collector to return to God; he would have to give up his profession, and also return a fifth of the embezzled money. What would then be left to him and his family except begging? Jesus allows us to see that his tax collector takes the hopelessness of his position fully into account. He doesn't even dare raise his eyes to heaven, and as a sign of repentance he beats his breast (Lk. 23,48). In his despair all that he is able to stammer out is half a verse from a psalm "God, be merciful to me a sinner." According to the prevailing religious law this man has no chance. But because God does not bother about this law, he is able to leave the temple as a "just man." The significance of this can best be expressed in a paradox. God says to this sinner: "you are not at all in order, and you acknowledge this. And *that's* why you are in fact, in order."

Jesus has nothing against the piety of the pious; he himself calls to mind what is written in the Book of Leviticus about striving after the perfection of the Heavenly Father (Mt. 5,48; compare Lev. 19,2). At the same time he emphasizes that only God represents the measure by which a man's behavior should be judged, and not the actions of others.

At first glance the difference between the Pharisee and the tax collector is immense; it is the difference between a giant spotlight and a weak, flickering, pitiful half light. In comparison with the brilliant rays of the sun in a luminous sky though, they both pale. In other words, the point of comparison is God, and only God. There is no essential difference between the two men before God. The Pharisee has no special *merits* to show for himself; he has merely done what is perfectly understandable according to his comprehension of himself; he has followed instructions. Such a person has no reason at all to make a lot of fuss; he "has only done what was his duty" (paraphrase, Lk.17,10).

If appearances do not deceive, the lesson in the parable has not been adequately understood even today, especially in church circles. Time and time again people confuse religious good behavior with virtue, and think of moral failures as depraved people. One overlooks too easily and too gladly that virtue does not represent the result of a constant struggle for holiness in every case; it is often merely a mixture of few opportunities and fear of social control. On the other hand, there are people who suffer from their questionable way of life to such an extent that they definitely cannot be described as immoral — whatever else they may be. Yet in church circles we are often tempted, and repeatedly fall prey to this temptation, to canonize the Pharisee and damn the tax collector to the deepest hell. I know of a case of a single mother; on the occasion of the christening of her child the priest said before all the relations present that he could not let the christening bell be rung "because the child is illegitimate." Naturally this woman never set foot in a church again. I also know of people who continue destroying each other slowly because church institutions close the door on them if it is known that their marriage failed years ago. Dignitaries given the status of civil servants force them to tell this lie because the facade must be preserved. If these people do separate (we are not even talking about divorce) because this is no kind of life, one takes away from them what they need to survive; their circle of acquaintances, their work, their profession....It seems that there are Christians who think that they can only remind others of the memorized sentences of belief if they give them an object lesson.

Jesus preaches against this sort of mentality that tries to classify others morally by their outward appearance alone. The people who only feel secure if they can cling firmly to the posts of the law, to the railings, to the crash barriers of church regulations, will of course confine themselves to interpreting the story of the Pharisee and the tax collector as a parable against self-justification; and they will waste no time thinking as to whether this attitude of self-justification might perhaps have psychological causes. If they were to pursue this question, they would presumably come to the conclusion that they need to make the comparison between themselves and those who do *everything* wrong, in order to confirm that *they alone* are on the right way. This certainty — constantly in need of self-confirmation — protects them from the knowledge threatening the whole of their concrete existence; that the stirring of feeling also has right on its side, not only the paragraphs of the law; that regulations cannot be dispensed by autonomous thinking and acting; that law has in no way the same significance as justice; that even the commandments are not our purpose and goal, but comparable only to guides or street signposts; and that other people sometimes *have* to go another way because the appropriate street, for whatever reason, is not practicable for them, although they are striving after the same goal. People like the Pharisee Jesus tells us about are never able to find a way to others. They are also *incapable* of understanding the other, because they can never turn as one person to another: Communication (if one may even call it that) always happens in an impersonal way: *one* must, *it* says, *the Bible* says, *the church* teaches.... they can never say *I* think, *I* mean, *I* am of the opinion that....

Paragons of virtue like the Pharisee can never be improved, with their white shirts and beautifully ironed pinstripe suits covering their souls; they are immensely further from God than the tax collector with his tortured soul and wounded heart.

Writers have always had more feeling for this than biblical scribes. We only have to remember Fyodor Dostoevsky, who ventured into the inner labyrinth of the human psyche. In his novel "Crime and Punishment" he created the character of the down-at-the-heels official Marmeladoff, the image of a hopeless alcoholic who has lost the last grain of self respect. He describes himself as "a sot" and says "I bear the mark of the beast."[11] So that he can indulge in his addiction, he even pawns the shoes, stockings and headscarf of his eighteen year-old daughter, who is forced to become a prostitute to support her three younger siblings. But Sonia, who even gives him her last thirty kopecks, with which he buys half a bottle of spirits, does not reproach him; she only looks at him silently. "She said nothing, but only gave me a look, a heavenly look, such as angels have when they weep over the faults of us men, but condemn us not! It is worse than being scolded." It is this pain that awakens an endless yearning for forgiveness and redemption in Marmeladoff.

"...but He who has had pity on all men and sees all hearts, will have pity on us; He alone is Judge......We shall all be judged by Him, and He will forgive us all: the evil and the good, the wise and the gentle.....And when He has finished with the rest, our turn will come too: "Draw nigh' He will say to us, 'draw nigh, ye drunkards, ye cowards, ye dissolute men.' And we shall draw nigh without trembling. And then He will say unto us 'You are sots! Ye bear the mark of the beast on your foreheads, yet come unto Me.' And the wise and intel-

ligent will say 'Lord, wherefore dost thou receive these?' And He will answer 'I receive them, O ye wise and intelligent men, because not one of them thought himself worthy of this favor.' And then He will hold out his arms, and we shall throw ourselves into them; and we shall burst into tears; and then we shall understand everything. All the world will understand....Thy kingdom come, O Lord."

One would not be doing justice to Dostoevsky's view if one were to interpret Marmeladoff's speech as simply the wild talk of a drunkard, who is on the edge of delirium. It is only because his understanding no longer permits him to censure his own thoughts, that the secret yearnings of this totally broken man gain admittance to his consciousness. In a state of sobriety, even the simple wish to be accepted by God somehow, would have seemed an illusion. Only drunkenness enables him to give expression to his last hope in a *miracle*: God does not wish to cast him out, in spite of his misery and depravity.

The drunkard's words allow us to empathize with a person who, expelled from society and despised by the "respectable," is finished and lives on the edge of the abyss. To the extent that one takes account of how tortuous the ways are that lead to such forlornness, one becomes skeptical of both judgment and condemnation, and also of the all too confining definitions of perfection and depravity.

In the character of Marmeladoff, Dostoevsky illustrates in a psychologically acceptable way, what Jesus maintains in his story of the tax collector and the Pharisee: that the holiness or sinfulness of a person cannot be judged by his outward behavior. It is not by reason of his "works" but only by the measure of his yearning for purity and attachment to God that the saint can be distinguished from the sinner. Of prime and sole importance is this yearning for God and for his proximity, which finds such piteous and therefore such moving expression in the tax collector's short prayer. Because of his attitude, this man is on the same plane as Mary, and at the same time placed at her side; in Luke's gospel it is clearly said of both of them that God has "exalted" them from their "low degree" (Lk. 1,52; 18,14).

Detours in the History of Theology

So it does not depend on "works" but on one's fundamental attitude; or in New Testament language: on faith. If professed Catholics prick up their ears here at a Lutheran undertone, they are not the victims of an acoustical error! But that does not mean that our interpretation of the parable of the generous vineyard owner and the example of the Pharisee and the tax collector in any way contradict Jesus's views.

It is true that Martin Luther saw an unholy and rampant justification of works in the Catholic church, and fought against it bitterly. It is equally accurate to say that the Council of Trent (1545-1563), along with the reformers, intended to emphasize a certainty of salvation so grounded in faith that it might have seemed that no significance at all would be granted to a way of life pleasing to God — in other words, to good works.

Both Luther's teaching and the reaction of the Council of Trent can only be understood if we turn our eyes back to the history of theology. The theologians of the Middle Ages defined faith predominantly as a rational affirmation of the truths of revelation (dogmas). [12] According to this understanding, faith is not of the will, but is an act of realization through which man acquires religious knowledge. But if the mere taking of God's revelation as true brings about salvation, there is no more reason to harangue over hell, as the unrepentant sinner can also agree with the statements of the holy scriptures. In view of this awkward situation, the theology of the Middle Ages was forced to differentiate between a *faith which is no more than rational acceptance of the truth of revelation,* (and therefore worthless) *and a faith to which something must come* so that it can bring about salvation. But what should make this faith "complete"? The answer is simple: the assent of reason, which expresses itself in "caritas," that is, in love. To put it more simply, according to the interpretation of the theologians of the Middle Ages, faith is only effective when one not only takes note of the truths of salvation, but also takes them to one's heart.

However, in Catholic theology, which Luther studied, love that should mold and form -— yes, even saturate faith -— had long before become *works* of love. It is true enough that the New Testament also says that true faith expresses itself in deeds (see Jas. 2,14). According to the understanding of the New Testament, good works, to a certain extent, are a "logical result" of faith, and thereby the concrete expression of an inner attitude. Popular preaching though, generally emphasized that a man could buy salvation with his works. In other words, faith no longer rescues man; he far more saves himself through his good deeds. Of necessity, Luther (and other reformers) had the impression of a self-satisfied, self-justifying "workshop" of faith. With the best will in the world, Luther could find no hint of this in the whole of the New Testament.

He taught the opposite: come to the point! The New Testament demanded no works as *conditions* of salvation; it expects them as a *result* of the salvation granted by faith, which will be given to man if he places his whole trust in God — remember the tax collector in the parable, who is "justified" (i.e. deemed good) as he pours out his heart to God (i.e. believes). This is what Luther means when he maintains that through faith alone ("sola fide") can salvation come about. In short, a person will not become good by reason of his own efforts. The opposite is true: only because he has first been justified ("made good") by God, can he do anything good at all.

It is known that Luther was never able to bring his theology into line with the passage in James's epistle according to which man "...is justified by works and not by faith alone" (Jas.2,28). But if one takes into consideration that good works, so to say, are a "natural" result of faith, then this is true, and is both good New Testament teaching *and* good Lutheran; the faith that brings about salvation.

Luther, incidentally, also saw himself forced to distinguish between two kinds of faith, between a *living* faith, and a *dead* faith. The latter occurs when someone believes that the experience of salvation handed down by the Bible is true, but does not allow himself to be inwardly touched by it. It also applies to people who believe that man can trust God unconditionally, without however, being able to take this step themselves, that is, without being able to believe in God.

"Now I have often spoken of two kinds of faith. The first you full well believe, that Christ is such a man, (a bringer of salvation) and that he preached in all the gospels, but you do not believe that he is such a man to you, *and you doubt whether you have such things from him or will have them, and you think, yes he is such a man to the others, like St. Peter and the pious saints,*

(yet) who knows whether he is also to me.... *This faith is nothing....it is a faith* from *Christ, and not* to *or* in *Christ.... This unholy and negative faith is now taught by the damned devils's synagogue, the high schools of Paris with their sisters, together with all the monasteries and all papists.*"[13]

On the other hand, according to Luther a living faith is present when a person links the biblical experience of salvation to his own sinful existence in unbounded trust in God, and applies them both to himself.

"The true faith, which is also alone the Christian belief, is when you believe without any wavering, that Christ is not such a man only to St. Peter and the saints but also to you yourself, *yes,* you yourself more than all the others. *Your sanctity does not lie in the fact that you believe that Christ is a Christ to the pious (a redeemer), but that in* you *he is a Christ and is* yours. *This faith makes that Christ lovingly pleasing, and he tastes sweet in your heart: then* love and good works follow without being forced. *But if they do not follow, then this faith is certainly not there. For where faith is, there must also be the Holy Spirit."*

Luther formulates his position trenchantly in another paragraph in a double thesis.

"If faith is not without all — even the smallest — works, then it does not justify; yes, such a "faith" does not even deserve this name. Indeed it is impossible that faith should not bring forth many eager and great works."[14]

Let us now look at the teaching decisions in the Council of Trent's decree on justification (1547), which was ostensibly aimed against the reformers' understanding of faith. There it is said that faith, understood as unconditional trust in God, is in no way enough to attain salvation. Faith is simply "the *beginning* of human salvation, the basis and the root of every justi-fication"[15] ...then if hope and love do not join faith, a man is neither perfectly one with Christ, nor does Christ make him a living member of his body. For this reason it is correct to say that faith without works is dead and futile" (DH 1531; compare Jas. 2,17.20) Besides, man must "turn himself towards God quite freely, believing that what has been revealed and promised by God is true" (DH 1526).

This "rejection" of the reformers' teaching leaves us rather at a loss today. The Council condemned the view that a faith without consequences — that is, not concretized in equivalent works — can bring about salvation. In the same way it rejected the opinion that the teaching of faith should be given a mere peripheral importance. But neither Luther nor the other reformers had ever preached that. And the opposite is also valid: the justification of works, against which Luther fought so vehemently, had never been put forward by the *theology* of the Catholic Church. On the contrary, the teaching decision of Trent shows clearly that good works are *the fruit and result* of faith, according to Catholic interpretation.

To get back to our theme: basically Jesus anticipated the whole of this theological controversy in the parables of the generous vineyard owner and the example of the Pharisee and the tax collector. But the church *procla-mation* had always made heavy weather of the teachings contained in them. And it would seem that Jesus's point -— in spite of all the burdensome theological confron-tations during the Reformation -— has never been fully received. So many men simply cannot believe that God's devotion is also there for them. This leads to their discovering in God exactly the same features that Kafka gave to his father. An example of this is Tilman Moser's autobiographical report "God's Poisoning," in which the author turns to God personally:

"I have to thank you for an experience of terrible dimensions; the feeling that I am depraved. I have been able to remain protected from this experience for some years and over a long period of time, but it overtakes me again in particular forms of loveless criticism. Then even until today, uncontrollable floodgates are opened in me, and it seems that you pour out this feeling from poisonous cisterns over me. Then I think: no one can ever love me, and in the deepest sense, my life is in vain. "[16]

Here God is addressed personally: but in reality the subject is a reckoning with those who have disfigured God's image to such an extent that it is unrecognizable. The extraordinary response to Moser's book after its publication can be explained by the many people who found their own problems addressed and voiced in it. This shows that at least for some the church proclamation has long been unable to bring the image of God in Jesus adequately to light.

But Jesus himself still endeavors to give us courage, and particularly those of us who eke out our lives far from God's instructions and promises. He deliberately avoids destroying the last remnants of any miserable self-confidence with threats. It is rather that Jesus himself is certain that only his joyful tidings of forgiveness can bring about repentance, and that those who are furthest from God will turn towards him again with all the more glowing hearts. In a short parable of only three sentences Jesus expresses his conviction of this.

"A certain creditor had two debtors; one owned five hundred denarii, and the other fifty. When they could not pay he forgave them both. Which of them will love him more?" (Lk. 7,41f).

Time and time again Jesus speaks of God's uncondi-tioned love for men. And whenever he speaks of it the word "merit" never crosses his lips. We can understand this, because God does not know any love that can be bought. Let me put it this way:

As the sun does not shine and the rain does not fall *because* the trees turn green and the flowers bloom, but *so that* they can grow and unfold in their full splendor, in the same way one must not understand God's love towards man as a reward for any kind of good works; rather God takes every man as he is, because only thus can the good within him take root and grow.[17]

3
Damned for all Eternity?

God is infinitely good. Jesus illustrates this basic theme of his proclamation in numerous parables. We must, however, face the fact that a few of his stories end ominously. At least they seem to hint that for a time the caring father of the prodigal son suddenly loses his patience. And in some stories the talk is of condemnation and rejection, of damnation and hell fire.

"A man had a fig tree planted in his vineyard; and he came seeking fruit on it and found none. And he said to the vine-dresser 'Lo, these three years I have come seeking fruit on this fig tree, and I find none. Cut it down; why should it use up the ground?' And he answered him, 'Let it alone, sir, this year also, till I dig about it and put on manure. And if it bears fruit next year, well and good; but if not, you can cut it down'." (Lk. 13,6-9).

Obviously Jesus is here thinking of the people of Israel who, in the Hebrew Bible, are repeatedly compared to a vineyard or a fig tree that carries no fruit: "When I would gather them says the Lord, there are no grapes on the vine, no figs on the fig tree; even the leaves are withered, and what I gave them has passed away from them." (Jer. 8,13; compare Hos. 9,10; Mic. 7,1).

The vineyard owner represents God; it must remain an open question whether Jesus sees himself as the vine-dresser in his parable. However, what is certain in this story is that he beseeches his fellow countrymen to repent; they can only avoid threatening divine judgment by doing so. But God still grants a last temporary reprieve; there is still the chance of turning all to the good. The fig tree will even have manure so that it can carry fruit, although this was not at all customary. It will not be God's responsibility if the tree is to be cut down.

As already mentioned, Jesus specifically visualizes his own people in this parable. In Luke, however, who was writing his gospel for converted gentiles and not for Christians of Jewish origin, the story acquires a universal and therefore exemplary significance.

God's forbearance is not in question. The weak and the despairing are comforted and told they can again find hope. But one cannot turn a deaf ear to the warning. The thought of God's goodness can indeed tempt us not to take him seriously any more, and so greatly endanger our own salvation.

Masters or Helpers?

In another parable, again about a vineyard, God appears as patient and yet at the same time as inexorably strict.

"A man planted a vineyard, and set a hedge around it, and dug a pit for the wine press, and built a tower, and let it out to tenants, and went into another country. When the time came, he sent a servant to the tenants, to get from them some of the fruit of the vineyard. And they took him and beat him, and sent him away empty handed. Again he sent to them another servant, and they wounded him in the head, and treated him shamefully. And he sent another and him they killed; and so with

many others, some they beat and some they killed. He had still one other, a beloved son; finally he sent him to them saying, 'they will respect my son.' But those tenants said one to another, 'this is the heir; come let us kill him and the inheritance will be ours.' And they took him and killed him and cast him out of the vineyard. What will the owner of the vineyard do? He will come and destroy the tenants, and give the vineyard to others." (Mk. 12,1-9; compare Mt. 21,33-41; Lk. 20,9-16).

A vineyard, a pit, a tower — this introduction sounded like a well known song in the ears of the listeners at that time, a song that the prophet Isaiah had sung a couple of hundred years earlier:

"Let me sing for my beloved
a love song concerning his vineyard
on a very fertile hill.
He digged it and cleared it of stones,
and planted it with choice vines:
he built a watchtower in the midst of it,
and hewed out a wine vat in it;
and he looked for it to yield grapes,
but it yielded wild grapes..."
(Is. 5f).

What happened further? The disappointed owner tore out the hedge and brought down the wall; the vineyard became a wasteland, trampled down by cattle and overgrown with thorns and thistles. The last stanza of the song contains the message:

"For the vineyard of the Lord of Hosts
is the house of Israel,
and the men of Judah
are his pleasant planting;
and he looked for justice,
but behold, bloodshed;

68

for righteousness
but behold, a cry!" (Is.5,7)

The accused here are the people of Israel; although chosen by God, they have proved themselves faithless and therefore depraved; a theme that was repeatedly stressed by the prophets in the face of the ruling injustice (compare Hos. 10,1; Jer. 2,21; Ezek:15,1-8), and that Jesus now seizes upon and develops in the parable of the rebellious tenants.

His listeners would have pricked up their ears. At least they could not possibly escape the fact that he had reinterpreted the image of the vineyard in an unusual, even outrageous way. But this is only apparent right at the end of the story. At first Jesus draws his fellow countrymen's attention to the owner of the vineyard. Jahweh, the God of Israel, is implied, there can be no doubt of this. The tenants who lease the vineyard represent the religious leaders. From the way Mark passes on this parable, it emerges that they take their task seriously and are aware of its importance. After Jesus has driven out the sellers and buyers from the temple, it is the chief priests, the scribes and the elders who come up to him and ask: "By what authority are you doing these things?" (Mk. 11,28). Instead of answering their question directly, Jesus tells them the story of the rebellious tenants. Naturally the temple theologians and the religious administrators grasp straight away that they and their predecessors are identified with the tenants. Were the "servants" — in short, the prophets — not persecuted, banished, gagged, subjugated, eliminated and liquidated by the religious elite? So the prophetic legends in circulation perhaps have a historic foundation. ("O Jerusalem, Jerusalem, killing the prophets and stoning those who are sent to you" (Mt. 23,37)). Does not Jeremiah

69

complain of his sad lot, and the fact that he is not the first prophet to waste his breath? (compare Jer. 7,25-28). At the same time the priests and students of the scriptures who are present understand that Jesus means himself by the "beloved son," finally sent by the vineyard owner.

Naturally because of their position the functionaries of faith also notice what the vineyard signifies in this parable which is so provocative, especially towards them. Now this image no longer stands for the chosen people, but for the *kingdom of God,* expected by the whole of Israel. All Jesus's mind and energies are focussed on this. The kingdom of God proclaimed by Jesus includes the human conception of laws which no longer stand contrary to God's justice. But Jesus makes this reproach to the high priests, scribes and elders who have forgotten that they are merely tenants and not owners of the vineyard. Although they are only there as helpers, they behave as masters; remember Dostoevski's Inquisitor!

No other writer before or after this Russian novelist has defined this problem with such depth as he did in his legend of the "Grand Inquisitor." It was no accident that he set the action in Seville in the 16th century, during the time when the Spanish Inquisition reached its tragic climax. His famous legend tells how Jesus determines to visit "his children only for a moment, and there where the flames were crackling round the heretics."[1] But as soon as he shows himself in the great square of Seville the Cardinal Grand Inquisitor, an old man of nearly ninety, has him taken to prison. During the night the Inquisitor comes to him, and hurls his fearful charges into the face of Jesus.

"For Thou hast come to hinder us, and Thou knowest that. But dost Thou know what will be tomorrow?...to-

morrow I shall condemn Thee and burn Thee at the stake as the worst of heretics.....I tell Thee that man is tormented by no greater anxiety than to find someone quickly to whom he can hand over that gift of freedom with which the ill-fated creature is born. But only one who can appease their conscience can take over their freedom.....how is the weak soul to blame that it is unable to receive such terrible gifts? Canst Thou have simply come to the elect and for the elect? But if so, it is a mystery and we cannot understand it. And if it is a mystery, we too have a right to preach a mystery, and to teach them that it's not the free judgment of their hearts, not love that matters, but a mystery which they must follow blindly, even against their conscience. So we have done. We have corrected Thy work....why hast Thou come now to hinder us?"

Because the freedom and the responsibility bound to it proclaimed by Jesus represent a burden for people, the Grand Inquisitor feels himself bound to improve upon Jesus's work. He takes away the "unbearable burden" of freedom. But in this way he puts himself in God's place. Here we are not interested in the fact that Dostoevski aims this reproach at the Catholic church, about which, as an Orthodox Christian, he had a completely distorted conception. What is far more relevant to our problem is the basic idea of the "Legend" embodied in the person of the Grand Inquisitor, namely, that the person who awaits definitive salvation by himself, of necessity raises the level of *his* concept of God and *his* religious ideas to a criterion of what brings salvation.

Just as the Grand Inquisitor brings his full power and authority to bear on domesticizing the gospel, so do the rebellious tenants seek to establish the kingdom of God according to their own conception. For this reason they plague and persecute God's messengers and kill the legitimate "inheritor." This means that the tragedy of our first parents is once again repeated — they wanted to decide for themselves what was good and evil; they wanted to be like God — and found themselves naked before the gates of paradise. Jesus wants to warn us of this in his parable. There is still a chance for his opponents: *if* you kill the son and usurp God's rule, thus adding further to your contrariness — and this time certainly more seriously — *then* the father will come and "destroy the tenants and give the vineyard to others." *Then the measure will be full.*

When Jesus threatens that the father will "destroy" the wicked tenants, it means that those who oppose God's rule against their better judgment definitively forfeit salvation.

Jesus shows how serious this is, and how seriously he himself takes it in a parable (only related by Matthew), which to a certain extent is a continuation of the parable of the tenants. This time the thought of justice is predominant.

"Again, the kingdom of heaven is like a net which was thrown into the sea and gathered fish of every kind; when it was full, men drew it ashore and sat down and sorted out the good into vessels but threw away the bad. So will it be at the close of the age. The angels will come out and separate the evil from the righteous, and throw them into the furnace of fire; there men will weep and gnash their teeth." (Mt. 13,47-50).

Here Jesus uses an image from the fisherman's life that was so familiar to his Galilean fellow countrymen, to describe the justice that will happen "at the close of the age." In catching fish a large trawl net, its lower edge secured down with stones, was stretched between two boats. During the voyage to the shore the two boats gradually approached each other. Finally the fishermen drew the net completely together and dragged it to the shore where, according to the instructions in the law of cleanliness (see Lev. 11) "the bad" were thrown away. Among these were "the swarming creatures of the waters" for example, prawns, and every sort "that has not fins and scales" (Lev.11, 10,12).

Both the events depicted, that is, the catching and then sorting of the fish, (where the "unclean" were destroyed) apply to two moments in the history of salvation. The first and now immediate phase is the time of the collection. Jesus sees his mission in leading God's original people of Israel back to Jahweh. But in doing this, he experiences that his followers are not simply made up of people searching for God and hungry for redemption, but that all kinds of pickpockets, idlers, and tramps have attached themselves to him — in fact dubious characters, for whom the thought of God's kingdom is as foreign as flying is to a goat. But it is not yet the time for separation; justice is still to come. There is still a chance of changing oneself.

Perhaps Jesus was aware that his comparison was a little inappropriate. In contrast to the good and the bad fish in the net, people are able to change. In fact, Jesus does say that people are capable of repentance. There is no doubt about this in the words he uses to describe the way to court, and to the judges.

"Make friends quickly with your accuser, while you are going with him to court, lest your accuser hand you over to the judge, and the judge to the guard, and you be put in prison; truly I say to you, you will never get out till you have paid the last penny" (Mt. 5,25-26; compare Lk. 12,58-59).

In both his parable of the fishing net and in the description of the way to the courts, Jesus turns to the indifferent and the skeptics, as well as to the spiritually blind and to those that have gone astray. They are all exhorted to change their lives fundamentally. In both parables, the main focus lies on the coming selection at the end of the age, on the division between the good and the wicked, on the *judgment*.

Most probably the interpretation of both texts and their threatening conclusions can be traced back to the evangelists (and this also applies to the parable of the rebellious tenants). But without doubt, the form told by Jesus contains a serious warning.

Belief in Heaven or Fear of Hell?

Unavoidably we are faced with an important question: Is God's goodness as limitless as some of the parables suggest? I recall the one of the housewife and the lost drachma, of the shepherd who loses one sheep and of the prodigal son. Doesn't Jesus also proclaim a two-faced God, whose mild countenance becomes dark with revengeful thoughts as soon as he sees that a person opposes his will and his directions? Doesn't Jesus's joyful message amount to a threatening message if we do not listen to him attentively enough? In the end, does he not perhaps even raise the fear of the flames of hell among men in order to secure their belief in heaven?

The opposite question: can we respect a person who says to us, "It's all the same how you stand in relation to me; actually it doesn't interest me"? I myself would prefer not to have anything to do with such a person. Basically he is saying to me "You don't interest me in the slightest." I would rather have someone scream at me "I'll stick by you, please believe this; in the end you can do what you want. But if you go on like this, I shall be furious with you. That you must understand."

I imagine it must be similar with God. Jesus's talk of the good, patient and endlessly merciful God is basically misunderstood if it leads to us making a chum out of a God who turns a blind eye to our going astray, to our taking life lightly and creeping away from all responsibility. God acts very decisively if something decisive is in the cards. And when one sees these things so, many seemingly unbearable statements in the Old Testament appear in a slightly different light.

Sometimes when Jesus also uses such a hard and decisive tone it is done because he is so concerned for the people's good. He gives them to understand that they are running into danger, passing life by, missing their goal. He pursues this view when he reminds us in the parable of the fishing net that the bad fish are thrown away during the sorting out. In the evangelist's interpretation this thought is even clearer "So it will be at the close of the age. The angels will come out and separate the evil from the righteous, and throw them into the furnace of fire; there men will weep and gnash their teeth." (Mt. 13,49f)

This way of speaking may well appear somewhat strange to us today, but only as long as we forget that Jesus is exclusively using the customary concept of hell that had developed and changed during the course of several centuries.

Before the Babylonian exile (586-538 BC) it was assumed that the dead led a shadow existence in Sheol (which means the land of nothing, a kingdom of the dead which men thought lay under the earth). As the belief in the resurrection gradually took hold during the 2nd century BC in Israel, this kingdom of the dead was considered a place of punishment for the godless. At the time of Jesus the thought of an "intermediate state" was widely spread. What was here implied was the time and space between the death of the individual and the last judgment of us all. The kingdom of the dead became a place of waiting for the dead before the general judgment. Those damned in this judgment were believed to sink into a burning lake of fire and sulphur (Rev. 19,20; 20,10) or into hell fire. The latter is also described in Mark's gospel as Gehenna (Mk. 9,43,45,47). This is the Greek word for Ben-Hinnom, the Hinnom valley lying to the south of Jerusalem. During the reigns of Ahaz (734-728 and Manasseh (699-643) children were burned there as offerings to God (see 2 Chron. 28,3; 33,6). This is why the prophets threatened judgment upon this valley, and why this later led to the assumption that one day hell fire would burst out there. Thus the name of Gehenna became synonymous with the concept of hell fire.

We have already said that these popular concepts and theological models of thought were also familiar to Jesus. That is why he speaks quite naturally of the "hell of fire" (Mt. 5,22) of the "eternal fire" (Mt. 18,8; 25,41; compare Mk. 9,43); of the "furnace of fire" (Mt. 13,42); but also of the "outer darkness," where "men will weep and gnash their teeth" (Mt. 8,12; 22,13; 25,30).

These statements seem to contradict one another. Fire and darkness cancel each other out. This itself shows us that these comments contain no worthwhile information about the nature of hell. However, the subject that both images share is what it finally comes to; those damned to hell are there where God is not. Accordingly, hell consists in the absence of God.

In church proclamations the horrors of hell were usually depicted with more enthusiasm than heavenly bliss. In his "Praise of Folly" Erasmus of Rotterdam (1469-1536) expressed his irony over this strange tendency among theologians: "They are happy too while they're depicting everything in hell down to the last detail, as if they'd spent several years there....."[2]

Jesus, on the other hand, (and this also applies to the authors of the New Testament) shows no interest at all in the topography of hell, and therefore this problem is completely irrelevant to us as well. An entirely different question is of far more importance: what is Jesus's purpose when he speaks of hell?[3]

We are most likely to find an answer when we examine the literary form of the corresponding statements more closely. In connection with his "preaching on hell" Jesus employs a means frequently found in the Hebrew Bible, and this is the prophetic threat. At the time when a preacher embellished his statements in this form, everyone knew immediately that he was not concerned to uncover future events for us, but wanted to bring us to our senses now, and move us to repent. To some extent one can compare these prophetic threats to the reprimands of a school teacher to an undisciplined pupil: "I'm going to send you out of the room!" This is not a factual pronouncement, nor is it a forecast; it is a call to order in the form of a threat. The teacher's intention is to remind the pupil that he must behave himself. If he does this, the point has been made.

Jesus's words on judgment and hell, passed down to us by the evangelists, have a similar ring. "I tell you, many will come from east and west and sit at table with Abraham, Isaac and Jacob in the kingdom of heaven, while the sons of the kingdom will be thrown into outer darkness; there men will weep and gnash their teeth" (Mt. 8,11f). Only the recognition of the literary form — the prophetic threat — ensures an adequate understanding of these words. We are not concerned with an infallible "to-be-fulfilled" forecast, but with a warning to comply with the invitation to belief, as long as there is time. Jesus does not want to proclaim ruin and damnation, he wants to call us to repent and follow him. And he does this with the thought concepts and methods of speech of the time.

Does this mean then, that hell is not to be taken seriously? This question intensifies when we remember that Jesus has proclaimed a loving and merciful God. Besides, we must consider why this God should have created men, knowing beforehand that they were going to shut themselves off from his love to such an extent that they would forever remain cut off from his company. Does not such an idea amount to thinking that God wants the ruin of mankind? If one excludes this, the thought must arise as to whether God's love, and therefore God himself, has not come to grief because of human evil.

These distressing thoughts amount to thinking that the simplest solution might lie in God's total destruction of the damned. But this idea seems completely foreign to Jesus, and this is also why the church has always emphasized the eternity of hell's punishment. In fact, we can scarcely imagine that God would suddenly no longer desire what he himself had called into being; a human creature made in his own image. Besides, Jesus emphasizes in his more comforting parables — we remember the woman with the lost drachma, the shepherd with his sheep gone astray, the prodigal son — that God loves a person, even when he has turned away from him completely. If we think this through consequentially, it implies that God himself would not be able to face the damned in hell with indifference, but would *suffer* with and for them.

Some theologians have tried to solve this particular problem with the aid of the so-called Apokatástasis teaching (from the Greek word *apokatástasis*, meaning re-establishment). In antiquity this was represented by some of the church fathers, particularly those within the circle of Origen of Alexandria (c. 185-254). According to this view, God could bring about the re-establishment of the whole of creation in an act of universal reconciliation, which would also affect the damned. As a result of this concept, hell could then be compared to a prolonged purification. In 543 this teaching was expressly condemned at a church council in Constantinople. "Whoever says or holds to the idea that the punishment of demons and godless people is temporary, and that after a certain time it will come to an end, that is, there will be a re-establishing of demons and godless people, shall be excommunicated with the anathema (i.e. banned from the church as a false teacher)."[4]

In the face of the terrible results of human evil, in fact, the thought of universal reconciliation proves to be more than just a great problem. Could we then take the sufferings of the tormented and the tortured, of those liquidated in the interests of others at all seriously? Would not the thought that God might finally forgive all seem, right from the start, to betray and deride the victims of human vileness? And what good would it do to talk about human responsibility if in the end it is all a matter of indifference?

But let us ask the question the other way round: can we still follow Thomas Aquinas when he teaches that the saved rejoice over the sufferings of the damned — not directly but merely "in so far as these sufferings are the expression of God's justice"?[5] Without doubt, the question of justice becomes sharper when it is asked precisely because of the victims. But doesn't the boundary between the joy over God's justice and the malicious joy over the lot of the damned appear very fluid? Is not the apostle Paul more convincing when he writes that he himself would rather forfeit salvation if in this way he could save his brothers and sisters? "For I could wish that I myself were accursed and cut off from Christ for the sake of my brethren, my kinsmen by race" (Rom. 9,3).

If then, precisely because of this statement, the thought of a final reconciliation is taken up anew, is it not (as in the case of the supporters of *universal* reconciliation) to be understood as meaning that *God of himself* would finally join everything together into one great harmony? If the subject here is final forgiveness, it happens *from the perspective of the victims.*

An example can best explain what is meant by this. There is someone whom I have deeply wounded through my behavior, and fully aware of my atrocious deeds, I ask him for forgiveness. If this person is then reconciled to me and forgives me, the experience is both joyful and yet at the same time extremely painful. For only in the face of the other's generosity can I become fully conscious of my vile behavior. It's rather like someone going into a heated room with frozen feet; at first he experiences great pain before the warmth can flow through his limbs. And so the reconciliation I have received can only begin to have its "effect" on me if I can comprehend and *myself* go through the entire pain that I have caused the other.

Here I want to ask a tentative question: is a cleansing encounter between the executioners and their victims at the time of death quite unthinkable?... Can we not see a starting point here in the New Testament? Does not Jesus speak up for his executioners when he says: "Father, forgive them for they know not what they do"(Lk. 23,34). And does not the dying Stephen pray for his murderers: "Lord, do not hold this sin against them" (Acts 7,60)?

The thought of such a mutual reconciliation, therefore, seems theologically worth considering, because it certainly does not contradict the God that Jesus proclaimed. It also does not play down the pain suffered, or diminish the victims because *it was they* who granted forgiveness and gave reconciliation.

Besides, here we must entertain the consideration that even those damned to hell for all eternity remain *God's children*; and how could God be happy about this? Is the idea completely bizarre that God himself will be "delivered" from his suffering if the victims forgive their murderers? According to Johannes B. Brantschen, to some extent this thought is fundamental to Jesus's parable of the merciful father and his two sons:

"The father is also lost *as long as his sons do not understand him, as love is always lost and suffers if it is not understood, and not answered. The father suffers as long as his sons remain unreconciled. The father's joy will only be complete, and love be re-established, when the eldest son is able to give his hand to his younger brother.*

Because God has bound himself to us — the folly of divine love — he has made himself dependent upon us; the reconciliation of his daughters and sons is also his joy. Do not the victims, God's darlings, wish to make God's joy complete?" [6]

Certainly Jesus unequivocally teaches that man can definitely forfeit salvation if he turns away from God or his messengers, and shapes his existence on his own authority. But when does a decision with such consequences happen? Here too — in the face of church tradition, I have to speak with a certain reticence but not with timidity — we may dare ask the question as to whether the divine encounter with judgment, precisely at the moment of death, could not be the "place" for man's last decisive and free act. Although this thought is not anchored in the scriptures, there seems to be nothing in them to contradict it.

At first glance it may seem as if church teaching about the eternity of hell's punishment, and thereby the very existence of hell itself, should not be questioned. If we do not imagine hell as a place, but define it as a state of absence from God, the talk of "hell existing" is indeed problematical. Generally this talk tacitly presupposes what one should be able to prove, but which cannot be proved at all; that there are people who decide against God in the most radical way, freely and consciously in their thinking and actions, and then adhere to this resolution. It is this attitude of extreme, irrevocable evil that Jesus warns us about when he speaks of hell. But whether anyone ever makes a basic decision of such consequence simply cannot be said. Without wishing to play down frightful human aberrations and their consequences, may one not ask whether people do not also become guilty because others are themselves guilty of lack of devotion and humanity towards them? In order to say with certainty that a person has desired his own hellish ruin and has therefore found it, one would have to know his last, deepest and innermost motives. These usually remain hidden even from the individual himself.

Judas — rejected for all Eternity?

In this connection some of Jesus's words about Judas are always quoted. They are found in Mark's gospel (which served Luke and Matthew as a model). "It would have been better for that man if he had not been born" (Mk. 14,21).

The interpretation of these words as a final rejection of Judas is completely arbitrary, and there are no grounds for it in the text. The relevant passage in Mark can best be understood if one compares it to a passage from Luke's gospel (Lk. 17,1f) which can also be found in Matthew (Mt. 18,6f).

Luke 17,1-2:

Temptations to sin are sure to come; but woe to him by whom they come. It would be better for him if a millstone were hung round his neck and he were cast into the sea.

Mark 14,21:

For the Son of Man goes as it is written of him, but woe to that man by whom the Son of Man is betrayed. It would have been better for that man if he had never been born.

Comparison of the texts shows that Mark has taken over a warning against offense (Greek *skándalon* = temptation or offense) from another source (compare Mk. 9,42) — that was also known to Luke and Matthew — and applied it to Judas's outrageous betrayal. According to this, although the statement condemns the traitor's terrible deed, it says nothing about eternal damnation, but simply contains the extremely serious warning not to match it and cause offense.

Incidentally, public feeling seems not to have come to terms with the thought that Judas might be damned for all eternity because of his act. In its own way the 10th century Irish legend of the abbot St. Brendan documents this. With a small group of monks he undertook a sea journey at God's bidding. One Sunday during the course of their seven year long journey the pilgrims come across a man squatting on a rock. Asked his name he replies:

"I am Judas, the traitor. Grace has brought me here, because of Christ's merciful will. This place is like paradise for me, however fearful the torments that wait for me again this evening . . . . . Every Sunday I have quiet here, and also on the days of Christmas until the Epiphany, from Easter until Whitsun, and also on the Feast of the Purification and the Assumption of Mary." [7]

Obviously the eternity of hell's punishment was at times considered unthinkable; this is why the legend actually allows Judas "periods of recovery." Augustine (354-430), in a short basic course in belief written for a certain Laurentius, entertains the thought that the damned, at least at times, (on Sundays?) were freed from their torments. [8]

On the other hand, it was Judas who served as an object of demonstration as far as hell was concerned, obviously because it was thought that the existence of hell could be inferred through him in a particularly plausible way. At any rate the Judas legends of the Middle Ages (their roots reach back to the apocryphal Arabian childhood gospel of the 6th century) united all thinkable ominous motifs in this figure from the Bible, myth and folklore. Even as a child Judas is obsessed by the devil; he commits fratricide, he is a robber; unknowingly he kills his father and incestuously marries his mother. [9] Obviously there was a tendency to stylize Judas as the prototype of the rejected sinner, and so safeguard the current opinion that such a monster deserved hell in any case, and therefore would most certainly be damned for all eternity. However, one or two witnesses document that this thesis was not accepted unquestionably. A sermon about this written by

84

St. Vincent Ferrer (1350-1419) in 1391 brought him into serious conflict with the Inquisition. At first this Dominican saint maintained that Judas, after his act, was seized by a "truthful and repentant cast of mind" and tried with all his strength to get nearer to Christ and apologize for his betrayal.

"But as Christ was accompanied by such a crowd of people on the way to Calvary, it was impossible for Judas to come to him, and then he said within his heart: as I cannot reach the feet of the Master, at least I will approach him in spirit, and humbly beg him for forgiveness. In fact he did this, and when he took the rope and hanged himself, his soul hurried towards Christ on Mount Calvary, and there asked him for forgiveness, and received this in abundance. He rose to heaven then with Christ, and so his soul enjoys blessedness among the chosen."[10]

Not surprisingly because of this view the Spanish Grand Inquisitor Nikolaus Eymerich instituted a trial against his fellow monk Vincent in 1394. However Benedict XIII — regarded by many in the confusion of schism at the time as the legitimate successor of Peter, and only later classified by historical research as an anti-pope — demanded that the records should be handed back, and burned them before the Inquisitor's eyes....

Here it is worth mentioning a 17th century hymn which warned the faithful against treating Judas as a scapegoat.

"O our great sins and heavy misdeeds
were conquered by Christ, God's true son
upon the cross,
so that we may not strongly curse
poor Judas and the Jewish crowds,
for true enough, the guilt is ours."[11]

On the other hand, the image of Judas from the Enlightenment until today is different. Rather like Friedrich Gottlieb Klopstock in his "Messiah" (1748-1763), writers following him have made an effort at explanation, which at least tries to understand Judas's act and thereby Judas himself subjectively.[12] The problem of his possible redemption here is understandably no longer so acute as in earlier times.

Although the church has always canonized only exemplary Christians, in her official teaching she has never maintained that a particular person has been damned to hell. The most that she permitted herself on this subject was the excommunication and if need be the colorful formula attending it[13] — through the ultimate exercise of her "power of the keys."

"Judge not, that you be not judged" (Mt. 7,1). In this connection these words from Jesus's Sermon on the Mount imply that no one may hope for salvation for himself without including all mankind in this hope. Unusual as it may seem at this point, Jesus's talk of hell belongs to the gospel proclaimed by him. This means that his sermon on hell does not aim at narrowing down his good tidings, but that his statements about hell should far more be evaluated and interpreted from the point of view of his good tidings. Then it also becomes clear what function his own speaking about hell actually has. He does not wish to threaten with sanctions for the next life, but to emphasize the seriousness of life here. He reminds us: you can gain everything or lose everything — and everything means God. Our life, Jesus says, must not go astray in a careless noncommitment. We must be mindful of our responsibility and our dignity.

Accordingly, hell is not simply a fiction which only serves to move people half-way towards a Christian life. But it is also no absolute reality, in that we cannot simply maintain that only one single person is "in hell."

It is rather an actual possibility that confronts every single human being throughout life. To put it concretely, there is indeed the possibility that I will deny God and my fellow human beings in such a way that nothing is left of me but my egoism. Jesus's good tidings and his redeeming action entitle us to the hope that no one ever experiences this most terrible of all possibilities. Yes, in fact God does desire "all men to be saved" (1 Tim. 2,4). And this hope for salvation must simply be greater than all fear of hell.

4

Of Expectations, of Disappointments, and of Success

There was once a time when the survival of man was almost entirely dependent upon two factors; upon the weather and upon the chance that he could carry out his arduous work in the fields in peace. Drought and weather catastrophes together with plagues and wars had a devastating effect upon the cycle of sowing and harvesting; starvation and mass deaths were the result. Memories of this lived on in the behavior of our grandparents, who found it virtually a sin to throw away a piece of bread. This reverence for bread has ancient roots. It goes back to the times during which people died in thousands after a bad harvest. It is therefore understandable that at the time of every sowing, people were not only filled with hope but also with anxiety. The conflict of these feelings is put into images by the psalmist:

"May those who sow with tears
reap with shouts of joy!
He that goes forth with weeping
bearing the seed for sowing,
shall come home with shouts of joy,
bringing his sheaves with him."
(Ps. 126,5f).

These lines remind us of times long past when the peasant walked behind his plough and arduously worked his fields by hand. In the meantime agricultural concerns have come largely to resemble industrial enterprises. However, the conflict of feelings that the psalmist describes is not so foreign to us today as might seem at first. In most of life's areas we fare very much like the sower. In the face of all our many efforts we can only hope that the success we expect will be forthcoming. And there is always the question, whether it is worth such investment.

Vain Investment?

This is the theme of the very first parable that Jesus tells, according to Mark's gospel.

"Listen! A sower went out to sow. And as he sowed, some seed fell along the path, and the birds came and devoured it. Other seed fell on rocky ground, where it had not much soil, and immediately it sprang up, since it had no depth of soil; and when the sun rose it was scorched, and since it had no root it withered away. Other seed fell among thorns, and the thorns grew up and choked it, and it yielded no grain. And other seeds fell into good soil and brought forth grain, growing up and increasing and yielding thirtyfold and sixtyfold and a hundredfold" (Mk. 4,3-8).

Even those not so well acquainted with the Bible are able to see that this whole episode bristles with inconsistencies. The thorn bushes and the path are on the edge of the field. It is likely that a few seeds might fall on them during sowing and the sower would probably not give it another thought. But surely no peasant is going to strew precious seed over a rocky field covered with a thin layer of soil; his grandfather would have told him

89

that he never wasted good seed like that when he was a young boy.

You don't have to have a diploma in agronomy to notice at once that in this story only the familiar image of the sower is drawn from life, while the episode described is completely foreign to reality.

It is easy to see the reason for this. The familiar image of the sower is not used so that a particular instruction can be derived from it. In fact the opposite is true: the basic statement is already established, and is then illustrated by means of an image from daily life. This is confirmed in the interpretation that follows the parable:

"The sower sows the word. And these are the ones along the path, where the word is sown; when they hear, Satan immediately comes and takes away the word which is sown in them. And these in like manner are the ones sown upon rocky ground, who, when they hear the word, immediately receive it with joy; and they have no root in themselves, but endure for a while; then, when tribulation or persecution arises on account of the word, immediately they fall away. And others are the ones sown among thorns; they are those who hear the word, but the cares of the world, and the delight in riches, and the desires for other things, enter in and choke the word, and it proves unfruitful. But those who were sown upon the good soil are the ones who hear the word and accept it and bear fruit, thirtyfold and sixtyfold and a hundredfold" (Mk. 4,14-20).

According to this interpretation, the people listening to the parable are at the center of the story. The pedagogical intention cannot be disregarded. The ignorant, who hear the word of God and ignore it, are warned; the changeable, who capitulate before the first difficulty, are admonished; the happy-go-lucky, who

lose their way in a hundred trivialities are exhorted....
in other words, the evangelist warns us not merely to
take note of God's word, but to clasp it to our hearts.

Does one necessarily have to interpret this parable
from the perspective of the readers of the time? Would
it not also be legitimate to think about the text from the
sower's point of view? The interpretation that follows
the parable suggests that this sower is not exactly in an
enviable position at the end of the story. Contrary to
expectation and against all experience, it seems that a
great deal, if not the greatest part of the seed, perishes.

What may appear rather unreal in the image seems
plausible as soon as one visualizes what is really being
described by the parable; that is, the early Christian
community. The greater part of the seed not growing
was an exception in the daily life of the peasant, but a
bitter reality within the Christian community. God's
word only brought about the desired effect among the
very few. Most people were indifferent to it.

Both the parable and its interpretation draw our
attention to the striking contrast that existed between
Jesus's proclamation and Jesus's successors. On the
other hand, we could assume that neither the parable
nor the interpretation can be traced back to Jesus, but
are creations of a community that had to come to terms
with the fact that the preaching of the crucified and risen
Lord had fallen upon deaf ears. This text reveals how
zealous Christians came to terms with their disappointment about this; that in spite of all their efforts inspiration within their own ranks was limited, and for the
most part those outside the community remained outside.

Seen within this background, the parable of the
sower suddenly seems to be threateningly topical. Instead of thinking about *sowing* and *harvesting* or *work*

91

and *yield*, we simply have to think of the categories we prefer today; *investment* and *success*, and then we recognize ourselves in the figure of this unfortunate sower.

Examples? An expert in ecology has invested a lot of time and money in an attempt to make people aware that mankind is poised upon the brink of an abyss. A college gets him to lecture, but he faces an almost empty hall, because so many of his contemporaries find the football game on television this evening more important than a discussion about the future chances for mankind. Or a pastor knows that not every sermon can be a bull's eye. But this time he has prepared himself particularly well because his theme lies very close to his heart — let's assume it's about the position of women in the church. When he does the rounds outside the church after the service, he gets absolutely no reaction from the men, and two lady parishioners give him to understand that women were really not created to play first violin, even in the area of the church; the music, as always, can be fully trusted to the organist; and besides, they came to church to take part in the service, and not to be confronted with the identity crisis of women's liberation.

All of us recognize this: you make a supreme effort, there is no lack of investment, and of course you believed in success and hoped for a positive resonance. And then comes the great disappointment. Other examples: many children during puberty and early adulthood can no longer affirm everything that was precious to their parents. They have other standards and shape their lives at their own discretion. The disappointed parents then ask themselves or others; have we done everything wrong?

Not everything. But some things. We should certainly allow ourselves to be questioned by sons and daughters. Perhaps we can even achieve the healing recognition that some of the things we have tried to pass on were really not worthwhile.

Of course the problem is quite different when parents have to recognize that in spite of all their intensive efforts and good intentions, their children are really "wayward" as the saying goes. Then they either despair or become resigned because they persuade themselves that all their efforts were in vain and simply not worth the trouble. But how does one know that with certainty? In contrast to nature, whose fruitfulness is bound to the cycles of the seasons, in man's heart a seed can sprout at any hour, and a plant grow from it. However much good will and pedagogical effort fall among thorns, on the path, or on thin layers of soil, whatever falls on fertile ground will germinate some day, grow, and develop. As the pouring rain can make the desert bloom, so can the heart of man be utterly changed when the moment we have waited for with such longing, but which we cannot control, comes, though it may come but once. All that lies in our power is to create the conditions, so that goodness can shine into the souls of our fellow human beings. But we may never *force* them to accept and absorb it. As we cannot control the moment when rain spills itself over the desert at last, so we cannot determine the day or the hour when our efforts will bear fruit. We are only entrusted with the sowing. All increase and success lie in God's hand alone.

"Grace is everywhere"

Georges Bernanos (1888-1948) did not just put this thought into words in his book "The Diary of a Country Priest"; he also gave it theological depth. [1]

The title tells us that the novel is the diary of a priest; he is young, inexperienced, and sickly. He works in a wretched and isolated village in Flanders. In his little parish which is "eaten up by boredom," he makes a bold but seemingly hopeless attempt to uncover the inaneness of conventional piety, and to expose the inconsistency between the institution of the church (that often functions as the servant of secular power) and the true Christianity which it professes to represent.

Naturally this simple priest knows how his fellow clergy judge him — for example the good-natured Curé from the neighboring village of Torcy:

"You're a queer specimen! I shouldn't think there's another softy like you in the whole diocese! And you work like a cart horse, sweating your guts out... Really His Grace must have been very hard up for priests to have given you the handling of a parish. Luckily a parish is solid enough — or you might break it."

The diarist is convinced of this himself:

"By nature I am probably coarse-grained, for I confess that I have always been repelled by the "lettered" priest. After all, to cultivate clever people is merely a way of dining out, and a priest has no right to go out to dinner in a world full of starving people...I am no longer fit to guide a parish. I have neither prudence, nor judgment, nor common sense, nor real humility."

This means: I am the wrong person in the wrong place. This is simply stated, and one does not have the impression that the priest is secretly hoping someone will contradict him. There is no sign of his flirting with his own humility, which can so soon turn into pride in displaying modesty. He is coming to terms with being nothing more than a useless servant, and what is superb — and moving — is that he does not despair because of it. His job is not the harvest, but the sowing:

"...nobody can see in advance what one bad thought may have as its consequence. Evil thoughts are like good ones: thousands may be scattered by the wind, or overgrown or dried up by the sun. Only one takes root. The seeds of good and evil are everywhere. Our great misfortune is that human justice always intervenes too late. We only repress or brand the act, without ever being able to go back further than the culprit."

In fact, human actions are sufficient to handle the secular interests of society. But it is left to God's power alone to transform the human heart. Bernanos's country priest expresses this insight in the short theological term "grace is everywhere." This knowledge is the sum of the experience of a seemingly unsuccessful priest's life — seen from outside. Is one obliged to develop it further, go deeper into it and so worry it to death?

"Grace is everywhere." This is the insight that lies at the foundation of the parable of the sower. It also applies to the interpretation of the parable (possibly added later) in which disappointment that Jesus's good tidings have by no means brought about the expected inspiration is clearly visible. But we should not merely be content with this analysis. Although the goal is far from being reached, we must not stop there. This, too, is reflected in the parable of the sower; there is no lecturing in its address to the lukewarm members of the community, but encouragement: let Jesus's words become effective in you! Open yourself to this experience! You will be astonished what his words can bring about in you, if you will come to terms with them seriously! Thus the parable bears impressive witness to the living hope which trusts in the word of God as proclaimed by Jesus and further spread by the community. It will seize hold of hearts and change the world; it will bring forth fruit thirtyfold, sixtyfold, yes, a hundredfold!

At the same time the central point of this parable becomes clear; it is neither the sower nor the listeners, but only the word of God, from which we can expect every conceivable effect.

The Effective Power of Words

Inevitably the famous scene in which Goethe's Faust struggles to translate the first sentence of John's gospel from the "holy original" into his own beloved German tongue comes to mind here.

> *"Written it is: in the beginning was the Word!*
> *My progress stops! Who helps me on?*
> *Value the Word so highly can I not,*
> *It must be rendered otherwise....."*

Obviously Faust does not think the "Word" is capable of much. The deed has more effective power for him.

> *"The spirit helps, at once I counsel find*
> *And comforted can write: in the beginning*
> *was the deed!"[2]*

But are not deeds first caused by words? And does not every deed itself represent a "speaking symbol," that is, a word? Words create new realities. They are able to awake human beings to a new life. They can also kill.

Someone says to another: "I don't want to have anything more to do with you. You don't exist for me anymore." These are death-bringing, fatal words, because they destroy human companionship. But the opposite is also true; one single true word of forgiveness is often able to heal the deepest wounds.

Some words shape us so decisively that they change the whole of our lives. A good example of this is found in Theodor Storm's novella "The Rider on the Grey Horse." After Hauke Haien has declared his love for the dyke reeve's daughter, they hold hands and go home. "The stars in the high heavens sparkled over the silent marshes; a light east wind blew, bringing severe cold with it; but the two went on without many scarves or garments on them, as if it had suddenly turned to spring."[3]

Francis of Assisi also discovered that words can transform one's life and set one in a totally new direction, when he gazed upon the image of the crucified Christ in the ruined church of San Damiano outside Assisi, and suddenly heard a voice within his heart: "Francis, put my house in order again!" It is well known that these words brought about one of the most far-reaching reforms in the church.

Is it then surprising that time and time again the Bible points to the effective power of words? It is not by chance that God's first act told of in the Bible is contained in words of creation: "And God said 'Let there be light'" (Gen. 1,3). Whenever God speaks he also acts. "For he spoke, and it came to be; he commanded, and it stood forth" (Ps. 33,9). God's word is creative. Without fail it causes what it announces. This belief in the effective power of God's word is anchored in the whole of the Hebrew Bible.

"For as the rain and the snow come
down from heaven,
and return not thither but water
the earth,
making it bring forth and sprout,

97

giving seed to the sower and bread
to the eater,
so shall my word be that goes forth
from my mouth;
it shall not return to me empty,
but it shall accomplish that which I
purpose,
and prosper in the thing for which
I sent it." (Is. 55,10-11).

The parable of the sower elucidates and supplements this text from Isaiah. It illustrates that God's word is infinitely stronger than all conceivable resistance. It will bear fruit thirtyfold, sixtyfold, yes, a hundredfold. To put it differently: we cannot stop the coming of God's kingdom.

Mark emphasizes this connection between *God's word* and *God's kingdom* in his gospel by handing down two further parables concerned with the growth of the seed *and* the spreading of God's word shortly after the parable of the sower:

"And he said, 'The kingdom of God is as if a man should scatter seed upon the ground, and should sleep and rise night and day, and the seed should sprout and grow, he knows not how. The earth produces of itself, first the blade, then the ear, then the full grain in the ear. But when the grain is ripe, at once he puts in the sickle, because the harvest has come'" (Mk 4, 26-29)

"And he said (further) 'With what can we compare the kingdom of God, or what parable shall we use for it? It is like a grain of mustard seed, which, when sown upon the ground, is the smallest of all the seeds on earth; yet when it is sown it grows up and becomes the greatest of all shrubs, and puts forth large branches, so that the birds of the air can make nests in its shade'"
(Mk. 4,30-32).

Matthew also relates the parable of the mustard seed (13,31f) and so does Luke (13,18f). Immediately following it they both relate a further parable which points in the same direction:

"And again he said, 'To what shall I compare the kingdom of God? It is like the leaven which a woman took and hid in three measures of flour, till it was all leavened'." (Lk. 13,20; compare Mt. 13,33).

The original Greek text speaks of an exact measure of "three seah," which has the capacity of almost forty liters, corresponding to nearly half a hundredweight of flour, an amount that would be enough to bake bread for about a hundred people.[4] Only the exact wording can reconstruct the actual meaning of the parable: God's kingdom embraces a dimension that simply goes beyond all human powers of imagination.

The parables of the growing seed, the mustard seed and the leaven also emphasize that God's kingdom is a pure *gift of grace:* just as the seed sprouts from itself, grows and develops, while the peasant goes about his daily tasks, just as the smallest of all seeds known at the time develops into a great mustard tree without man's help, and just as the leaven turns the flour without the housewife doing anything about it, so will God's kingdom become reality of itself, if people will only hold their hearts open to it.

In contrast to the parable of the sower, these three later parables belong to the authentic *proclamation of Jesus.* Presumably Jesus had those doubters in mind who were skeptical of his preaching about the coming of God's kingdom.

At the time of Jesus the rabbis were discussing whether God's kingdom would come at all; and the parables we have mentioned attempted to answer this question. At the time of the evangelists on the other hand, the early Christian community was asking itself when God's kingdom would take shape at last. In connection with these altered questions the parables naturally underwent a new interpretation, because the thought of the kingdom of God could only be seen together with the spreading and growth of the church.

A Warning against Rash Judgment

This point is clearly seen in the example of a radical change that Matthew carried out on Mark's text (which served him as a model together with a written collection of Jesus's preachings).

Instead of simply taking over the parable of the sowing (Mk. 4,26-29), Matthew puts another parable in its place, presumably going back to traditional stories known to him and others at the time.

"The kingdom of heaven (= kingdom of God; corresponding to rabbinical custom Matthew paraphrases God's name with the concept of "heaven") may be compared to a man who sowed good seed in his field; but while men were sleeping, his enemy came and sowed weeds among the wheat, and went away. So when the plants came up and bore grain, then the weeds appeared also. And the servants of the householder came and said to him, 'Sir, did you not sew good seed in your field? How then has it weeds?' He said to them 'An enemy has done this.' The servants said to him 'Then do you want us to go and gather them?' But he said 'No; lest in gathering the weeds you root up the wheat along with them. Let both grow together until the harvest; and at harvest time I will tell the reapers, Gather the weeds first and bind them in bundles to be burned, but gather the wheat into my barn'." (Mt.13,24-30).

100

A couple of hints should smooth access to this text. The linguistic formulation fosters the misunderstanding that God's kingdom is here compared to the sower; but the point of comparison is the harvest and the division of weeds and wheat that this involves. At first it seems surprising that the householder, against all custom, insists on not tearing up the weeds. Here another look at the original Greek text will help us; there is written *zizánia* (sing. *zizánion*). This signifies the plant known botanically as *Lolium temulentum,* which is darnel. During its early growth darnel looks like wheat; if it is weeded out it is very easy to pull out the wheat shoots as well. Later, when it is possible to distinguish between the two plants, their roots have already become so enmeshed together that the weeding out of the darnel can again cause damage to the wheat. It is therefore reasonable to let both grow. When the wheat has ripened, the shearers let the darnel dry out so that they can then burn it, while the wheat is bound into sheaves. The division first comes at the time of harvest. God's kingdom is compared to this, and not — as one wrongly assumes — to the sower.

There are seemingly no difficulties in interpreting the parable; according to the evangelist's text, Jesus himself explains it:

"He who sows the good seed is the Son of Man; the field is the world, and the good seed means the sons of the kingdom; the weeds are the sons of the evil one, and the enemy who sowed them is the devil; the harvest is the close of the age and the reapers are angels. Just as the weeds are gathered and burned with fire, so will it be at the close of the age. The Son of Man will send out his angels, and they will gather out of his kingdom all causes of sin and all evildoers, and throw them into the furnace of fire; there men will weep and gnash their

101

teeth. Then the righteous will shine like the sun in the kingdom of their father. He who has ears, let him hear!" (Mt. 13,36-43).

This interpretation has unmistakable allegorical features. Each one of the seven elements in the story (sower, field, good seed etc.) refers to something quite particular. It almost certainly does not go back to Jesus, but to the evangelist. It reveals many of the evangelist's linguistic peculiarities, characteristic of the narrative parts of his writings.[5] So Matthew re-interprets the parable of the weeds and the wheat into a statement about the last judgment. He then puts this interpretation into Jesus's mouth.

But how did Jesus himself understand this parable? Did he want to warn his own people to anticipate God's final judgment that takes place at the moment of death?[6] Does he represent the view that the purity of God's people must be safeguarded by the exclusion of sinners?[7] Is the parable really concerned with the basic theological question as to whether God can stand by idly and see how evil prospers in the world and injustice triumphs?[8] Each answer to these questions says something, but all of them have the disadvantage that they are merely concerned with hypotheses that cannot be sufficiently supported by the text. What is definite is that the parable of the weeds and wheat originally contained the statement that the growth of God's kingdom takes place under the conditions of *this* world, in which good and evil prosper side by side.

For his part, Matthew associates the growth of God's kingdom with the developing early church, and at the same time indicates that there would have been some open and probably hotly debated questions within the early Christian community (we can no longer reconstruct them today) about the final realization of God's kingdom.

The parable is susceptible of wide interpretation. At the same time it is intriguingly explicit and timeless. The evangelist seems to suggest that we should learn to live with questions in certain areas of our religious behavior because some answers are far from obvious — we must search for answers slowly and laboriously. May we not infer that he would make the same suggestion for the church today?

The advice to let weeds and wheat grow side by side until the harvest does not mean that individual believers should be indifferent to good and evil, or that the difference between right and wrong is without meaning. Instead it reminds us that, as Georg Baudler says, it belongs to man's end and his mortality "that in this earthly life one cannot say or establish with absolute or objective certainty, either for oneself or for another person, whether one is good or bad."[9] Such final judgment belongs to God alone. An exegesis to this parable is developed in the famous exhortation that Paul gives to the Christians of Corinth: "Therefore do not pronounce judgment before the time, before the Lord comes, who will bring to light the things now hidden in darkness and will disclose the purposes of the heart" (1 Cor. 4,5; see Mt. 7,1).

Not only the individual believers but also the leaders of the community are warned not to take final judgment into their own hands. Only Matthew's (secondary) interpretation identifies the workers in the parable with the angels of judgment. As we have already seen, the story originally urges restraint in passing judgment. But very early on, the growth of the church was drawn into the interpretation. At this time (before Matthew wrote) those members of the community who held some kind of function as leaders could be identified with the responsible workers. They are emphatically warned by the householder — that is, Christ — not to make themselves lords over good and evil by coming to bold decisions about pending questions that have need of further clarification.

Even the most short sighted of Christians today can no longer overlook the burning importance of this admonition and its relevance for church leaders.

On November 21 1964 the second Vatican Council ceremoniously proclaimed the "Dogmatic Constitution on the Church: *Lumen gentium.*" This important text, wrestled with for a long time, replaced the earlier predominantly legalistic image of the church with the image of the church as the new people of God, thus underlining the character of the church as a *community* of faith. But this new and yet ancient view of the church (rooted in the gospels) fell increasingly into oblivion a good decade and a half later, especially among church leaders. In the meantime only slightly more dialogue and communication between church leaders and the rank and file can be felt, and participation of the latter in matters of decision seems not only undesirable, but almost impossible. Apparently many church leaders believe that the faithful are uninformed and that clergy who disagree are also in need of instruction. The outstanding ecumenical scholar Heinrich Fries expresses this in a somewhat more refined way: "in the whole church today we experience a consolidation of all authority and direction into Roman safekeeping which takes almost everything in the Church under its control. Unity in (even legitimate) diversity is seen as a danger."[10]

Unity is again increasingly understood as standardization in the sense of uniformity. In order to achieve this, only those bishops are named who can be expected to make the faithful march in step. In the early church, people were vividly aware that no one could fill the office of bishop unless the community wanted him. Pope St. Leo the Great (440-461) established the principle, "He who wishes to preside over all must be elected by all." But as a result of the interference of secular princes, the pope laid claim to choosing bishops himself; in such a situation, of course, this was a blessing. Although there is no longer any danger today of secular leaders interfering, Rome continues to insist on the right to appoint bishops in an absolutist manner." [11] This frequently leads not only to tension but to division among the faithful. Even these bishops seem not to be trusted. When it comes to appointing theology professors, this is no longer (as it was earlier) the prerogative of the local bishop, but now is the right of the apostolic chair, or more precisely, the Congregation for Catholic Education which consents to the appointment (one which has already been made) of theology professors by the theological faculties. [12] Rome reserves the right to withhold its consent (the "Nihil Obstat") without stating any reasons. [13] Theologians who signed the Cologne declaration — "Against incapacitating the Church — a Plea for an open Catholicism" — need have no great hopes of a teaching chair, however outstanding their qualifications may be. This is because every objection in Rome is interpreted as dissidence. Anyone with a counter question about Roman declarations is suspected of disloyalty, even if he can prove that his objections are relevant. The Roman authorities seem to have a tendency to confuse orthodoxy with conformism. Does this not lead people into the temptation of saying "yes and amen," simply so as not to endanger their own careers? Or do we merely accept possible dishonesty and hypocrisy by saying to ourselves that it is not important what a theologian *thinks*, but what he *publicly represents*?

To avoid any misunderstanding: of course truth is not "democratic"; it cannot be determined by means of a majority decision. But one can just as little determine truth absolutely by decree. If impressions do not deceive, church dignitaries as a rule seem to know already where truth lies and where error — and to forget that the *finding* of truth usually represents an extremely wearying and complex *process*. We only have to remember the crisis of modernism that reached its height at the beginning of the century (and from which we appear to have learnt precious little). Most of the representatives of this movement (Alfred Loisy, George Tyrrell, Ernesto Buonaiuti, etc.) tended to reduce the supernatural character (grace) of faith to an inner experience belonging to the nature of man, a mistake that was rightfully condemned. As a consequence, those who took up the basic question of the relationship between grace and nature, or more precisely between supernatural revelation and its historical and therefore temporal form of appearance (church teaching itself had no ready answer to this) made themselves the suspects of modernism. To take up an image familiar to us: when the representatives of church teaching decided that some theologians sowed weeds into the wheat, they panicked, lost their heads and devastated the whole field. The same drama was repeated in the 1950's, when predominantly French theologians (Henri de Lubac, Marie-Dominque Chenu, Yves Congar) quite reasonably discussed matters of modernism that no one had come to terms with. This resulted in the disparaging words "Nouvelle Theologie" coming into circulation. "The Sanctum Officium Sanctissimae Inquisitionis" (the Holy Office of the most

Holy Inquisition), at the time the relevant body for the teaching of faith, did not take the urgency of the questions posed by these theologians remotely into account; the unchangeableness *and* the historicity of truth, the relationship between nature and grace, the problem of cognition of God, and the interpretation of truths of belief. Instead they were all suspected of heresy; they were not even given a short hearing, but were removed from their teaching posts by means of disciplinary measures *without* any procedure. Although even in Rome today there is no doubt at all that great injustice was done to these outstanding seekers, the church's teaching body has never been sensitive enough to apologize to them officially and publicly for its discriminatory measures.

The seed, however, has sprouted. These theologians especially are among the actual forerunners of the Second Vatican Council, which as a result took up and examined in depth a large number of the themes they had addressed.

Among other things, this Council emphasized that the church in this world and time is always *on the way.* Referring to God's people of Israel wandering through the desert, it is said of the church that she "advances in this present era in search of a future and permanent city" (compare Heb. 13,14).[14] As long as the church prays for the coming of God's kingdom she has not reached her goal; she is on the way; and there is always the chance that she is on the wrong track, or has been led astray, or has taken a detour. Naturally this does not only apply to moral behavior, but refers just as much to the development of her teaching. No one doubts that God's spirit will bring the church towards his truth, and maintain her within it. But that does not imply that this truth simply drops into her lap; on the contrary, tireless exertion and continual wrestling for clarity are the indispensable requirements for the spirit of God revealing truth to his church, and maintaining her within it.

If this seems unclear to some of us, it presumably means that we are unfamiliar with church history and the first great crisis of the new church.

We know that at the time there was much discussion as to whether gentiles who had converted to Christianity had to be circumcised "according to the custom of Moses," and whether this circumcision was necessary for them to "be saved" — a view that some Jewish Christians from Judea held in their discussion with Paul and Barnabas (Acts. 15,1). It should be noticed that this was not just another pious custom, but the question as to whether circumcision represented an imperative requirement for attaining salvation. After "no small dissension and debate" (Acts. 15,2) about this matter, Paul and Barnabas go towards Jerusalem with some companions, presumably between 47-49 A.D., to seek the advice of the apostles and the elders of the community. On the occasion of this "Council of Apostles" there is again "much debate" (15,7). That is presumably putting it mildly: after all they are people from the Mideast debating against each other.

It is not only the theological significance of this incident that makes Luke handle it so fully. Obviously in his report he also intends to explain to his readers how they should proceed among themselves if questions of belief come to debating point. Neither Peter, the first of the apostles, nor James the Younger, highly respected in the original community in Jerusalem, act with authority. It is not a simple question of decreeing, but of argument. Luke obviously takes it for granted that the process of finding the truth should provoke debate. Attention should also be given to the fact that, according to Luke, it is not Peter but James, who has the last word in this intense discussion.

This does not suggest that the representatives of the church teaching body should in any way be denied the right to intervene in questions of faith; that is their task and their duty. But they should not encourage the bad habit of intervening in theological discussion *on a dogmatic level*, before all sides have been listened to, and all the arguments brought forward by the theologians have been discussed. The past has shown us how easily this kind of action can become a disaster. In such cases a *pastoral* statement is the most helpful course to take. In practice this means that the teaching body, instead of imposing rash sanctions upon theologians or condemning them, should make *the faithful as a whole* aware that theological discussions serve to discover truth — and that such a discovery of truth always needs time and can never proceed without difficulty.

The Second Vatican Council proclaims something which should be self-evident, namely that "the teaching body does not stand above the word of God but serves it."[15] If one really believes that God's word will assert itself in spite of all resistance, there is no doubt that this will have an effect on the way one copes with unusual views. These need not be wrong only because one has never confronted them seriously enough for whatever reason — out of a lack of spiritual mobility, intellectual lethargy or limitation? Or because of pure fear of what is "new"?

Once more it is Luke who teaches in the Acts of the Apostles how a wise man faces such issues. When the members of the high council decide to kill the apostles for arousing the people, the highly respected Pharisee and teacher of the law, Gamaliel, probably a grandson of the famous Hillel, comes forward to speak. With the help of two historical examples he reminds his colleagues that movements springing from merely human ambition must resolve themselves sooner or later. And he continues: "So in the present case I tell you, keep away from these men (the apostles) and let them alone; for if this plan or this undertaking is of men, it will fail; but if it is of God you will not be able to overthrow them. You might even be found opposing God!" (Acts. 5,38f). In other words; *let all grow until the harvest!* This attitude puts the Pharisee Gamaliel closer to Jesus than some of his own representatives.

So long as there are people who are driven here and there by hunger for "hearing the words of God" (Amos. 8,11) these words will win through, in spite of all resistance.

According to Christian opinion, *Jesus himself* is God's word that points the way (see Jn. 1,14). According to the New Testament, Jesus once compared himself to a seed. "Truly, truly I say to you, unless a grain of wheat falls into the earth and dies, it remains alone; but if it dies, it bears much fruit." (Jn. 12,24). This interpretation could be from the fourth evangelist; but it corresponds fully to the way Jesus sees himself.

Anyone who has looked at a field of wheat will always be astonished by the unbelievable strength with which the sprouts shoot out of the ground, and at the ears of grain that develop. A germ of wheat is a fearfully small thing in comparison to a tractor, that can crush the ears and destroy them. But the strength of the small germs that "die" in the earth are stronger, because they carry life within them.

If Jesus is to win through finally in spite of his death, then the reason is that he confirmed his whole preaching by his living. The same thing happens when people not only admire Jesus, but also try to follow him. Whenever

110

Christianity has asserted itself with force (in crusades, wars of religion, the Inquisition) it has betrayed Jesus's instructions. It is not by jumping headlong into the battle but only by offering the patient witness of faith lived that the miracle of the harvest can come about after man has sown in this fashion. The harvest, nevertheless, always remains a gift from God.

5

The Bridge upon which Man and God Meet

"Once upon a time there was a peasant woman, and a very wicked woman she was. And she died and did not leave a single good deed behind. The devils caught her and plunged her into the lake of fire. So her guardian angel stood and wondered what good deed of hers he could remember to tell to God; 'she once pulled up an onion in her garden' said he, 'and gave it to a beggar woman.' And God answered: 'You take that onion then, hold it out to her in the lake, and let her take hold and be pulled out. And if you can pull her out of the lake, let her come to Paradise, but if the onion breaks, then the woman must stay where she is.' The angel ran to the woman and held out the onion to her. 'Come,' said he, 'catch hold and I'll pull you out.' And he began cautiously pulling her out. He had just pulled her right out when the other sinners in the lake, seeing how she was being drawn out, began catching hold of her so as to be pulled out with her. But she was a very wicked woman and she began kicking them. 'I'm to be pulled out, not you. It's my onion, not yours.' As soon as she said that, the onion broke. And the woman fell into the lake and she is burning there to this day. So the angel wept and went away."[1]

This legend comes from Dostoevski's novel "The Brothers Karamazov." It is told by a young woman,

112

Grushenka, who judging from her experiences, would seem to look back over a good half century, but in fact she is only twenty-two.

After the death of her lover, a tyrannical widower, she is pestered by old Karamazov, a rake and a drunkard of the worst sort. Just to while away the time she is already involved with this man's son. Simultaneously she desires his younger brother Alyosha, a twenty year old novice in a monastery. One day she invites him to her house with the firm intention of seducing him. But it seems that she does this less from sexual desire than from a wish to revenge the earlier humiliations she has suffered. She was seduced by an officer at the age of seventeen, and then almost immediately abandoned by him. In the meantime this officer's wife has died, and he discovers that "this sensitive, injured and pathetic little orphan" has "become a plump rosy beauty of the Russian type." He lets her know that he intends to come for her. Is this the wish for compensation, is it longing, or even something like love, or is it simply curiosity, the desire for a fleeting adventure?

Grushenka believes that Alyosha despises her, and her revenge will consist in her dragging him down to her, so that before he can turn round he will find himself on a level with her, surrounded by the filth of life and full of disgust with himself: "He despises me...he won't even look at me...I wondered at myself for being so frightened of a boy. I'll get him in my clutches and laugh at him."

The Onion

In fact Alyosha expects to come face to face with a wicked person when he visits her; he has only seen her a few times and then fleetingly. And yet his gaze is untroubled because he does not despise her, and is therefore able to discover hidden traces of human goodness in her face: "I came here to find a wicked soul...I've found a true sister.....You've raised my soul from the depths."

She has raised *him*? When Grushenka hears this, she describes it as the first and only good deed of her life. Suddenly she is aware of a feeling unknown to her previously, of not being *quite* superfluous in this world. She says of herself: "...though I am bad, I did give away an onion."

She then tells Alyosha the legend of the onion. Obviously she is convinced that her own history is reflected in it. In her meeting Alyosha, she discovers that she is also a human being, and not the whore that everyone believes her to be. A gleam of the light that Alyosha spreads about him falls upon her face. As the angel in the legend draws up the wicked woman, so Alyosha draws Grushenka up to him; it seems that the onion continues to hold. Later we find out who is hanging onto Grushenka's feet, and how she reacts.

There is a parable in the gospels which has such similarities with Grushenka's legend that they cannot be overlooked.

"Therefore the kingdom of heaven may be compared to a king who wished to settle accounts with his servants. When he began the reckoning, one was brought to him who owed him ten thousand talents; and as he could not pay, his lord ordered him to be sold, with his wife and children and all that he had, and payment to be made. So the servant fell on his knees, imploring him, 'Lord, have patience with me, and I will pay you everything.' And out of pity for him the lord of that servant released him and forgave him the debt. But that same servant, as he went out, came upon one of his fellow servants

who owed him a hundred denarii; and seizing him by the throat he said, 'Pay what you owe.' So his fellow servant fell down and besought him, 'Have patience with me, and I will pay you.' He refused and went out and put him in prison till he should pay the debt. When his fellow servants saw what had taken place, they were greatly distressed, and they went and reported to their lord all that had taken place. Then his lord summoned him and said to him, 'You wicked servant! I forgave you all that debt because you besought me; and should not you have had mercy on your fellow servant, as I had mercy on you? And in anger his lord delivered him to the jailers, till he should pay all his debt. So also my heavenly father will do to everyone of you, if you do not forgive your brother from your heart" (Mt. 18,23-35).

Both stories, Jesus's parable of the hard hearted debtor servant and the legend passed down by Dostoevski of the heartless woman, are about people who are totally given over to egoism and self-centeredness. Both narrators give us to understand that God's will to salvation is bound to fail in such cases, because God cannot save anyone who denies his fellow human beings and turns away from them.

But there is no doubt about God's incomprehensible mercy in both cases. The legend tells us that he is even prepared to free the woman from the lake of fire, out of which, in fact, no rescue is possible. And the debt that the lord is prepared to waive — we can imagine the servant as a high official — is so enormous that the plea for deferment of payment, and the promise to pay it off, actually produce only one reaction in us: a roar of laughter. Naturally the lord knows that he will never get his money back, and that the request for postponement springs from pure despair. Contrary to all his expectations, the defaulter is not punished, but pardoned. Instead of giving him more time to pay, the lord waives payment. His goodness goes beyond all expectations.

Both the parable and the legend from Dostoevski's novel state that a person can be given a completely unhoped for chance that he has not *deserved*. In religious terms we are here speaking about grace.

The Principle of Grace

The concept of "grace" does not have a particularly good ring to it today. We no longer live in a feudal society, but have well-defined claims that we are entitled to by law. For our part, we do our utmost not to owe anyone anything. In no way do we want to rely on the "gracious" — that is condescending — attitude of others; we do anything to avoid this.

Therefore is it so surprising that more and more people believe that life is *graceless*? And this is the case, when it is not a fellow human being who counts, but only one's own interests. In a graceless society there are any number of laws, rules of behavior, and regulations, and one has to abide by these; pardon is never lovingly bestowed. What counts is performance, and anyone who has not learned to assert himself falls by the wayside. One man's bread is another man's death. Devour or be devoured. No one can go against this law of nature. So it is said.

This shows us what graceless actually means: ruthless, unfeeling, heartless, inconsiderate, merciless — all these together. Grace is the opposite of them all.

The fear of having to rely upon others corresponds to our endeavors to do everything through our own strength. Both these elements make us blind to the fact

116

that in the end we are indeed dependent upon our fellow human beings — and will remain so. We can't even thank ourselves for our own lives. Everything that makes life beautiful and bright — devotion and a feeling of security, friendship and love, trust and forgiveness — cannot be obtained through some kind of legal regulation, but are always a gift. Do not those moments of thanking a person from a full heart count as some of the happiest in our lives? In such situations we see with great clarity that life can only develop under the influence of grace. As light and water and warmth can bring a dying plant to bloom again, so a free "debtless" turning towards another can also alter a person fundamentally.

In contrast to the plant however, which blooms in silent beauty and does not boast of her magnificence, we seem to have a tendency to guard jealously what is given to us as our own property. We all too easily forget that everything that we claim for ourselves alone divides us from others, and only that which we can share with or communicate to our fellow human beings binds us to them.

Dostoevski's legend allows us to see that the angel would have been able to pull the woman up to paradise, even when the other sinners were hanging on to her. Only at the moment when she makes an effort to kick these away from her ("I'm to be pulled out, not you. It's my onion, not yours") does the onion break.

It is a similar situation with the servant in the parable. At the moment when he destroys his debtor, his own ruin follows. Both, the heartless woman and the hardhearted servant, act as if they had a right to that which they have received without deserving it.

117

Forgiveness as a Process

People are only able to find themselves by holding themselves open to grace. And their rescue is only assured when, for their part, they show mercy (grace) towards others. This knowledge lies at the foundation of both the story of the wicked woman and the parable of the debtor servant. Both stories rest on the conviction that, although God's mercy is inexhaustible, his readiness to forgive has limits which are not based upon his will, but upon the nature of the response. To put it rather drastically: Can one expect of God that he should pull violently up to heaven one who carries the devil within him and spreads hell around him?

Incidentally, the parable of the hardhearted debtor servant forms an answer to Peter's question which comes just before it: "Lord, how often shall my brother sin against me, and I forgive him?" (Mt. 18,21.) In his story Jesus reminds us that such a question is superfluous in itself whenever a person turns his gaze inward, and reflects how much he himself constantly relies upon God's mercy.

Here, if not sooner, people confronted with this problem will come forward with a couple of reservations, which are only too understandable. If a gross injustice is done to us, it is not so easy to forgive. If need be, we try through a pure act of will to forgive all the humiliation we have suffered. A sympathetic pastor, perhaps not particularly experienced in psychological matters, would presumably say that this is quite enough, as in the end, it is a question of good will. But this answer is not satisfactory because it does not take feelings into account: we know that when our heart is as full of anger and feelings of revenge as before, in

118

spite of the *will* to be reconciled, we simply *cannot forgive.*

There is no doubt that the gospels make anyone who follows Jesus aware of certain ideal norms of behavior. In this respect they are able to change a person's *way of thinking* while his *feelings* remain uninfluenced. Applied to our example: the mere *will* to forgive is in no way identical to *forgiveness itself.* If we remember that man is not a static but a dynamic being we cannot view forgiveness as a single, so to say isolated human act, it must rather be understood as a *process.*

Dostoevski was not only a great writer. He also had a great knowledge of the human soul and can probably help us here more than a shelf of text books of moral theology that are sometimes rather out of touch with life.

When Grushenka finds out one day that her widowed seducer wants her to go to him, she is at first completely at a loss. Although the affair was five years ago, she still has not been able to cope with the fact that this man took her so lightly and then made off. Of all people, she now asks the novice Alyosha, totally inexperienced in matters of the heart, for advice:

"And now that man who wronged me is come; I sit here waiting for a message from him. And do you know what that man has been to me? Five years ago, when Kuzma brought me here, I used to shut myself up, that no one might have sight or sound of me. I was a silly slip of a girl; I used to sit here sobbing, I used to lie awake all night, thinking: 'Where is he now, the man who wronged me? He's laughing at me with another woman, most likely. If only I could see him, if I could meet him again, I'd pay him out, I'd pay him out!' At night I used to lie sobbing into my pillow in the dark, and I used to brood over it, I used to tear my heart on purpose and

119

gloat over my anger. 'I'll pay him out, I'll pay him out!'
That's what I used to cry out in the dark. And when I
suddenly thought that I should really do nothing to him,
and that he was laughing at me then, or perhaps had
utterly forgotten me, I would fling myself onto the floor,
melt into helpless tears, and lie there shaking till dawn.
In the morning I would get up more spiteful than a dog,
ready to tear the whole world to pieces.....tell me, do
I love that man or not? the man who wronged me, do I
love him or not? Before you came, I lay here in the dark,
asking my heart whether I loved him. Decide for me
Alyosha, the time has come, it shall be as you say. Am
I to forgive him or not?" "But you have forgiven him
already," said Alyosha, smiling. "Yes, I really have
forgiven him" Grushenka murmured thoughtfully.
"What an abject heart! To my abject heart!" She
snatched up a glass from the table, emptied it at a gulp,
lifted it in the air and flung it on the floor. The glass
broke with a crash. A little cruel line came into her
smile. "Perhaps I haven't forgiven him though" she
said, with a sort of menace in her voice, and she
dropped her eyes to the ground as though she were
talking to herself. "Perhaps my heart is only getting
ready to forgive. I shall struggle with my heart. You
see, Alyosha, I've grown to love my tears in these five
years....perhaps I only love my resentment and not
him...."

How is it that Alyosha can tell this woman that she
has already forgiven her seducer? Only because every
single sentence that she speaks about him leads to the
conclusion that basically she loves him. But in conflict
with this attitude are her bad experiences, the insults
she has endured, the humiliation she has suffered, the
degradation, the countless nights of weeping, in fact the
whole pain that she has not been able to cope with. One

would certainly not be making a mistake in saying that Grushenka represents an almost too ideal figure of identification to all those who have had to endure similar bad experiences in their relations with others. But also in relationships that are not so dramatic, we again find ourselves in situations in which we become aware of the borders of our readiness to forgive (or our *possibility* to forgive). It is then particularly that we feel the need or even a kind of compulsion to punish someone for some insult or other, especially when we are particularly fond of them. We know that we should make the first move towards reconciliation; but does not logic often fall by the wayside when feelings and emotions are involved?

In his parable of the heartless debtor Jesus explains in a fundamental way that God's forgiveness is dependent upon our turning towards our fellow human beings, and the realization of this is also expressed in the legend of the onion. Going beyond this, Dostoevski reflects on the psychic mechanisms that work in man. He sketches a case study in Grushenka's fate which shows that forgiveness is not to be understood as a single act of the will, but, as a rule, the result of an extremely wearisome and painful process.

We do ourselves and our fellow human beings poor service if we simply repress insults and injustices suffered. We should first of all work through them. Then without any doubt, faith will activate the readiness to forgive, without canceling out the effective psychic and emotional laws of nature in the area of relationships between people. To put it traditionally: Grace does not take the place of nature, but presupposes it. No one needs to have a bad conscience if they cannot immediately forgive injustices done to them from one moment to the next. Those of us who are able to do so should ask ourselves: have we not perhaps become completely indifferent to a person whom we can forgive lightly? For the closer we feel ourselves bound to a person the more deeply are we wounded by wrongs inflicted upon us.

True reconciliation is really only possible if we are able to talk to the other about injuries suffered without anger and with a modicum of composure. The wounds may well heal; scars can remain.

Forgiveness is always a matter of trust, and this trust is absolutely necessary for rebuilding, as a condition for a possible reconciliation. Trust is given anew when one can say to the other, "I can count on you again, entirely. I believe that you mean it seriously." It is not important how quickly one forgives the other, but what is important is how intensively one works towards reconciliation. Where reconciliation happens, a bridge is built over the many chasms that open up so often between us poor human beings. And this bridge is the one place where God waits for us and where we can meet him.

6
Love Alone is Crucial

Religious legends are not often artistically success-ful. This is because their origins are based on their need to edify rather than to establish a claim as literature. But this does not imply that they are less "true" than accounts of real events.

Religious legends are an expression of meetings with the saint, the divine, or with God. Their truth can only be perceived when we inquire into their deep layers of meaning.

Jerusalem is Everywhere

Leo Tolstoy's story of the "Two Old Men" in his collected tales is a good example of this.[1]

"Two old men agreed once upon a time to go and pray to God in old Jerusalem. One was a rich muzhik, called Efim Tarasuich, the other a poor man called Elisyei Bodrov."

Quite some time has passed since the two old men took their vow, but Efim simply cannot find any time to fulfill it. First of all he has to arrange his grandson's wedding, then he wants to wait for his son's return from military service; and besides, he has started to build a new house. But Elisyei pushes him, and finally they set off upon the long road to Jerusalem.

Elisyei leaves home cheerfully and with a light heart, while Efim is plagued by a thousand worries that refuse to leave him alone. After five weeks they reach the Ukraine. One day Elisyei has such a burning thirst that he goes towards a deserted hut to ask for a drop of water. Efim walks on; his companion will soon catch up with him. Elisyei goes into the hut to be met by a horrifying sight: weeping children, a dying woman, a weakened peasant and a mortally ill farm-hand, all at the point of starvation. Elisyei goes to the next village, buys grain, flour and bread; he will stay here this day. In the meantime Efim has had a siesta, and thinking that his friend has overtaken him, he continues his pilgrimage.

The next day Elisyei kneads bread, and cares for the sick; but what will these people live on when he has gone? He pays off the mortgage on the field, buys the peasant a horse and a scythe, and whatever else he needs for his work. He now has only seventeen of his hundred roubles left, and twenty kopecks. There is nothing that he can do but turn his face homewards again. When he arrives he tells them that he got behind Efim, and lost all his money.

"'Forgive me for Christ's sake.' And he gave his old woman the remainder of the money. Elisyei asked about household affairs. Everything was well, they had done all it behooved them to do, there was no waste in the housekeeping, and they had all lived in peace and harmony."

In the meantime Efim reaches Odessa, crosses the sea, goes on to Jaffa with the other pilgrims on the ship, and after three days he manages to get to Jerusalem. At last he can go to divine service in the Church of the Holy Sepulchre. He finds room right at the back.

"There stood Efim, praying and looking straight into the chapel where was the very Sepulchre, and above the Sepulchre burned thirty-six lamps. There stood and looked Efim, when through his head flashed the thought 'What wonder is this?' Beneath the very lamps, in front of them all, stood an old pilgrim in a coarse cotton caftan, and he had a shining baldness all over his head, just like Elisyei Bodrov. ''Tis much like Elisyei' he thought; 'but it cannot be he. He could not have arrived here before me. Another ship does not follow us for a whole week. He could not have come on so quickly, and he was not on our ship. I saw all the pilgrims.' While Efim was thinking thus the old pilgrim bowed low three times; first he bowed before God, and then he bowed to the orthodox worshippers on both sides of him. And when the old man turned his head to the right, Efim recognized him at once. 'Tis he indeed, Bodrov; his beard is blackish and curly, and a little grayish on the tips of the whiskers. And the brows, and the eyes, and the nose — all the features are his. It is Elisyei Bodrov's very self.'

Efim rejoiced that his comrade had come, and marvelled how Elisyei could have got there before him....

And Efim kept good watch lest Elisyei should escape him. And now the mass was over, and the people began to move; they went forward to kiss the cross, there was a press and a throng, they came in the direction of Efim....and he began to force his way through the crowd so that he might get outside. He got outside, and went and went, and sought and sought for Elisyei and he went right out of the church, and yet he did not meet him."

As Efim begins his homeward journey after six weeks, he has not only seen the holy places, without doubt he has also witnessed a miracle. But we can only find out what he has really seen if we press forward into the deeper levels of this pious legend. A few days after they left home together, Elisyei succumbed to temptation, and took out his horn snuff box. To Efim's reprimand he replies with disarming openness; "My sin hath gained the upper hand.. what can I do?."

And it is Elisyei, of all people, who has given up the challenge, whom Efim sees when he goes into the Church of the Holy Sepulchre (and later he sees him twice more) "under the very lamps," while he, who has taken his vow seriously and fulfilled it conscientiously, is just "jostled aside." Efim goes to all the holy places; Bethlehem and Bethany and the Jordan. He asks for masses to be said for the dead, he buys candles, a bottle of holy water from the Jordan, and a handful of earth from the Holy Land to take home with him. But while doing all these pious exercises his thoughts circle constantly around domestic matters, and when he gives a rouble to another pilgrim who has been robbed, the suspicion that this man is a swindler gives him no peace.

Obviously this legend shows that although Elisyei was never in Jerusalem, he has in fact reached his goal, whereas Efim's way to God is obstructed by insuperable hindrances. He must have done something wrong. It so happens that on his way home Efim asked for a drink of water at the same hut that Elisyei visited before. And as the people there tell him about the unknown man who rescued them from death a year before, Efim becomes thoughtful.

"'My feet were indeed there' he resumed, 'but whether my spirit was there, or rather the spirit of another'...But this one thing he now understood: it is the will of God that everyone here below should work off his debt of sin by love and good works."

The miracle? It was not Elisyei that Efim saw in the Church of the Holy Sepulchre kneeling under the lamps by the holy fire. What he actually saw was that even the most pious can become sanctimonious hypocrites, if their religious efforts simply amount to an internalization or an externalization of faith — and that both false attitudes can certainly coexist. When faith is internalized, we forget that the gospel has to be realized by turning our gaze towards fellow human beings. Faith is externalized on the other hand, when we seek edification in rites and rituals, the audible recitation of prayers, the observation of commandments, in other words when we concentrate upon the means, thus missing the goal which is God himself. In short, an externalization of faith happens where religion becomes a means to an end, and God, if you look at the matter carefully, becomes almost superfluous.

It is well known that the older Tolstoy became a bitter critic of the Russian Orthodox Church. Nevertheless, one must agree with him that religion *can* be one of the many hindrances that separate man from God, and block our way to him.

Efim stands for all those pious people who miss what is crucial in their religious enthusiasm; they place great emphasis upon form and cling to formulae; they never take into account that this is merely a kind of insurance contract that is not countersigned.

Furthermore, the crucial clauses are missing from this contract. All genuine religious effort must involve not only God but our neighbor as well. Elisyei does not think of holy water from the Jordan, nor about candles; he places most importance on keeping a couple of miserable peasants from starvation. This is the deed that earns him his place under the nearest lamp, close to the sacred fire.

127

Jesus examined

In many ways Tolstoy's legend of the two old men reminds us of one of the most famous of Jesus's parables, the story of the Good Samaritan.

"And behold, a lawyer stood up to put him to the test, saying 'Teacher, what shall I do to inherit eternal life?' He said to him 'What is written in the law? How do you read?' And he answered 'You shall love the Lord thy God with all your heart, and with all your soul, and with all your strength, (Dtn. 6,5) and with all your mind; and your neighbor as yourself.' (Lev. 19,18) And he said to him 'You have answered right; do this, and you will live.'

But he, desiring to justify himself, said to Jesus 'And who is my neighbor?' Jesus replied 'A man was going down to Jericho, and he fell among robbers, who stripped him and beat him, and departed, leaving him half dead. Now by chance a priest was going down that road; and when he saw him he passed by on the other side. So likewise a Levite, when he came to the place and saw him, passed by on the other side. But a Samaritan, as he journeyed, came to where he was; and when he saw him, he had compassion, and went to him and bound up his wounds, pouring on oil and wine; then he set him on his own beast and brought him to an inn, and took care of him. And the next day he took out two denarii and gave them to the innkeeper, saying 'Take care of him; and whatever more you spend, I will repay you when I come back.' Which of these three, do you think, proved neighbor to the man who fell among robbers?' He said 'The one who showed mercy on him.' And Jesus said to him 'Go and do likewise'" (Lk.10,25-37).

The story from which this parable stems is of prime importance. A qualified lawyer (teacher of theological law) asks a lay theologian about the conditions for eternal life. Or even more than that: he *examines* him. It is clearly said that the lawyer intends to put Jesus on the spot. Jesus points to the law with a counter question and knows in advance that the Rabbi will quote the two famous texts about God's love (Deut. 6,5) and love for one's neighbor (Lev. 19,18) from the Hebrew Bible. In confirming the lawyer's answer Jesus takes over as the inquisitor. Even slow thinkers among his listeners would understand who has become the teacher here. Moreover, Jesus reminds us that theological knowledge can only lead to salvation if it touches our consciences: "Go and do likewise!"

There was no doubt that every Jew knew that one should love one's neighbor. There were many contemporary interpretations of the Torah which saw love of neighbor as one of its basic principles. The Talmud tells us about "one from the nations" (that is, a Gentile) who wanted to learn all the teachings during the period of time when he could stand on one leg — within a very short time! Rabbi Hillel, one of the most distinguished representatives of Pharisaism just before anno Domini, said to him "Do not do to your comrades what you would find hateful if it were done to you! This is the entire teaching. All the rest is your interpretation! Go and learn!" (Shabbat 31a).[2] Rabbi Hillel was most likely referring to a passage from the Book of Tobit (apocryphal to the Jews) which was written c. 200 BC, probably in the Aramaic language: "And what you hate, do not do to anyone" (Tob. 4,15).

Who counted as a "comrade" or "fellow human being" was disputed and there was also argument about those to whom one was *not obliged* to show the duties of the commandment to love. Love for one's neighbor was first of all to be directed towards one's own people: it was only in relation to them that the taking of revenge and harboring anger were forbidden: "You shall not take vengeance or bear any grudge against the sons of your own people." The instruction that follows immediately afterwards "but you shall love your neighbor as yourself" (Lev. 19,18) was only applied to one's own; it was not understood as an invitation to universal human love. At the time of Jesus almost all the rabbis supported this nationalistic interpretation.

However, the book of Leviticus contains the instruction that the foreigner who is living on Jewish ground "shall be to you as the native among you" (Lev. 19,34). Pointing expressly to Israel's bad experiences in the past ("for you were strangers in the land of Egypt" Lev. 19,34) it follows that the commandment to love should be applied without differentiation to all strangers settled within the community. But several rabbinical witnesses from the 2nd century AD verify that these directions were interpreted in an extremely restrictive manner, even at the time of Jesus;[3] not all the foreigners living in the country at the time were implied, but only the proselytes, that is, those strangers (gentiles) who had been converted to Judaism. Furthermore it was required of them that they converted to the Jewish faith *totally*. According to Rabbi Joseph Ben Judah, who was teaching in 180, a proselyte who did not "take to heart and treasure the smallest word from the statutes of the Holy Scriptures" no longer counted as one of the people. This meant that one was not bound to apply the love commandment to him.

In no way does Jesus question the law; but he suggest that its *interpretation* is questionable. Does it not contradict the nature of the love commandment if one simply limits it to particular groups of persons, thereby making love cliquish and exclusive.

Proceeding from this question, Jesus tells a story to show that all the abstract considerations of the interpreters of the law are absurd. In order to do this, he chooses a scenic route that was very well known to his listeners; the road running between Jerusalem and Jericho.

The difference in altitude between the towns is remarkable, Jerusalem being 750 meters above sea level and Jericho 250 meters below. The road, almost thirty kilometers long, goes through a desert among deeply fissured rocks, where bands of thieves and robbers have hidden for centuries. Raids were not exactly the order of the day, but meetings with bandits and partisans were not unusual. Anyone who took this road certainly ran a risk.

At Jesus's time, many temple servants and priests had their residences in Jericho. His listeners therefore could well imagine that the priest was perhaps travelling home after his weekly duties in the temple. We are not told from which direction the Levite — a kind of temple servant — came. It is merely established that both of them see the man beaten half to death by the footpads, and pay no attention to him at all. It is possible that the priest was in a hurry to get home because he had to give a lecture in Jericho on the newest theological treatises circulating in Jerusalem at the time on the commandment to love, while the Levite was completely immersed in a pious meditation on the virtue of mercy.

Whatever it was that moved the two to avoid the wounded man, it is the third figure, now entering the scene, who is important, if only because he is necessary to the story. We might think that it would now be the turn of an ordinary Jew, at the worst an *am ha-ares*, an ignoramus from the lower stratum of society, who does

131

not go to synagogue and does not know the law. If this had been the case, this parable would be making an anti-clerical point. It would then be understood as a polemic against the keepers of the temple, and primarily against the priests.

However, the fact that the third man is a Samaritan, of all people, speaks against such an interpretation. And it is he, of all people, who takes on the wounded man. (By the way, his medical knowledge leaves something to be desired, because he puts healing oil on the wounds first, and then disinfects them with wine). Finally the anonymous stranger puts the anonymous wounded man on his beast, takes him to the next inn, and provides him with all possible care. We can imagine that the Samaritan is probably a merchant who commutes between Jerusalem and Jericho; in any case he assures the innkeeper — who obviously knows and trusts him — that he will cover any outstanding costs when he returns.

Jesus wants to show us a real act of love. But there is a little snag; the man who does this praiseworthy deed is a *stranger*, and above all, a *Samaritan*. It couldn't be more controversial.

There is a statement that comes down to us from Rabbi Eliezer, who was teaching c.90 AD: "He who eats the bread of the Samaritan is like one who eats pork, that is, unclean" (Shebith V111, 10)[4] Moreover the Talmud has many rabbinical discussions which deal with how far a Jew may go with a Samaritan. The general tenor of the replies: at best not at all. Jews and Samaritans were historically archenemies. In 721 BC Samaria, which lay between Galilee and Judea was taken over by the Assyrians (see 2 Kings 17,5). Later the mixed race known as the Samaritans sprang from the Israelites who remained behind after the conquest, and the newly arrived colonials. When the Jews who returned after the Babylonian Captivity turned down the Samaritans' offer to aid them in the building of the temple (Ezra 4,2f), the latter erected their own temple on the mount of Gerizim in the 5th century BC (it was destroyed in 129 BC). As a result, an independent cult and religious practice flourished among the population there. This caused the final break. In contrast to the Jews, only the five books of Moses were considered holy scripture by the Samaritans. Their hope of a Messiah was based upon a prophet at the end of time, from whom they expected the proclamation of the true teaching (compare Deut. 18,15. 18; Jn. 4,25).

The author of the deuterocanonical Book of Sirach (c. 190 BC) even then had nothing but scorn for the Samaritans: "I despise two races, and the third is no race; the dwellers on Mount Seir, the Philistines, and the foolish people (the Samaritans) who live in Shechem (Sir. 50,25f).

There are numerous examples in ancient Jewish manuscripts of this animosity between Jew and Samaritan, which also existed at the time of Jesus. There were often cases of the Samaritans molesting Jews who went through their country to make pilgrimages to Jerusalem.[5] Since the time when the Samaritans strewed bones about the temple during the Passover between 6-9 AD, thereby deliberately polluting it, an irreconcilable hatred existed between them and the Jews.

Because Jesus chose a Samaritan of all people, as an example of honorable behavior, he forfeited the sympathy of the lawyer who had provoked him into this discussion of the commandment to love. At the same time, he illustrated quite unmistakably that love towards a fellow human being should have no bounds. The priest and the Levite represent the law and cult, while the

Samaritan embodies the call to love. The unknown man fallen among thieves reminds us that law and cult are worthless if they do not serve to turn our gaze towards our suffering fellow human beings.

No New Demand

Was Jesus the first person to extend the commandment to include all persons? Among Christians this view is widely held. In fact, it seems that at Jesus's time hatred towards foreigners posed no moral problem. "You have heard that it was said, You shall love your neighbor and hate your enemy" (Mt. 5,43). But as we have already established, it was hotly disputed as to what was meant by your "neighbor." However the positive invitation (or instruction?) to hate your enemy is — at least in the formulation Matthew gives us — not supported by sources. It is possible that it was represented in the teachings of the Qumran community at the time of Jesus. Qumran, on the north west bank of the Dead Sea (where the famous Dead Sea Scrolls were found in 1947) was the domicile of a Jewish religious movement whose members lived in a monastic-like society. In one of the scrolls found there, the "sons of light" were expressly called upon to hate the sons of Belial (or "the sons of darkness").[6]

But this deals with a demand that was never represented in official Judaism. Certainly the Jewish prayer book contains some "cursing psalms" in which those praying had to curse their enemies, and call down all possible maledictions upon their heads: "May his children be fatherless, and his wife a widow! May his children wander about and beg; may they be driven out of the ruins they inhabit!" (Ps. 109,9f; 58,7-11; 129,5-8).

Incidentally, one must remember that the cursing of enemies in the antique world was widespread, that the languages of the Mideast tend to passionate utterance, and yet other scriptures expressly warn against repaying evil with evil. ("Do not say, 'I will repay evil.'" Prov. 20,22). Besides, at the time of Jesus, Judaism certainly obliged no one to hate and curse an enemy or an adversary. The Qumran community and other small groups were the exception.

Quite to the contrary, there are some instructions that expressly require one to help an enemy when he is in need: "If you meet your enemy's ox or his ass going astray, you shall bring it back to him. If you see the ass of one who hates you lying under its burden, you shall refrain from leaving him with it, you shall help him to lift it up" (Ex. 23,4-5). Or: "If your enemy is hungry, give him bread to eat; and if he is thirsty, give him water to drink" (Prov. 25,21).

The concept of love for your neighbor and love of your enemy developed in the parable of the Good Samaritan is therefore not at all new. It is rather that Jesus goes back to instincts and legends that had perhaps been suppressed or forgotten in the Judaism of the time, but were now being brought strikingly to the attention of his countrymen once again.

Incidentally, in practice Christianity has also failed to follow the teaching of Jesus. Let us remind ourselves of the unbearable maledictions that were linked to excommunicating one of the faithful in the Middle Ages:

"By the authority of Almighty God........we excommunicate and curse this thief or evildoer, and we banish him from the threshold of God's holy Church, so that for his torment he shall be seized by everlasting punishment.....May he be cursed wherever he finds himself,

at home, in the field, on the road, on the field path, in the forest, in water, in the church. May he be cursed when he dies, when he eats, when he drinks, when he hungers or thirsts, when he fasts, when he falls asleep, when he stands, when he sits, when he lies, when he works, when he rests, when he pisses, when he shits, when his blood is let. May he be cursed in all the members of his body. May he be cursed inside and outside (here all the parts of the body are counted, beginning with the hair and ending with toe nails)......May he be cursed in all the ligaments of his limbs, from the crown of his head to the soles of his feet may there be no health in him. May Christ, the Son of the living God, with the whole power of his majesty curse him; may heaven rise up against him with all the might that it moves in order to damn him, if he does not do penance and give satisfaction. Amen, so be it, Amen!"[7]

It should be noticed that we are here concerned with an official liturgical formula. Considering false teachings and mistaken ways of behavior, indisputably the church had the obligation to state publicly that one should be excluded from the community because of these. But she should never have so dishonored herself as to curse those in error — and in so brutal a fashion. When the excommunication formula ends by invoking — of all persons — Christ, the Son of the Living God and the teller of the parables of the Prodigal Son and the Good Samaritan, we are proving that the church then, as well as now, is subject to the danger of distancing herself from the gospels.

In the parable of the Good Samaritan Jesus reminds us that the commandment to love your neighbor goes beyond all national frontiers and ideological boundaries, and is also valid for those who think and believe other than we do.

Just how radical Jesus's treatment of the commandment to love is, is shown in an inconspicuous detail that we often overlook. The lawyer proceeds from the question "who is my neighbor?". Jesus corrects this at the end of his teaching: "Which of these three, do you think, proved neighbor to the man who fell among robbers?" We are never asked who is my neighbor and whom I am obliged to help. Instead *I myself* must prove a "neighbor" towards anyone who is dependent upon my help.

"Go and do likewise" Jesus encourages the *teacher* of the law. In fact, whatever one says about God's love, love of your neighbor, or love at all, proves empty talk, unless one can recognize one's father and mother in God, and in every man one's brother or sister. Wherever this happens, the kingdom of God proclaimed by Jesus comes tangibly nearer. It is not through sprinkling Jordan water or lighting candles that one finds one's way to the silver lamps in the Holy City, but only through selfless love for one's suffering fellow human beings.

Better Stories than Stage Directions

Again Jesus reminds us of this by telling a story:

"When the Son of Man comes in his glory, and all the angels with him, then he will sit on his glorious throne. Before him will be gathered all the nations, and he will separate them one from another as a shepherd separates the sheep from the goats, and he will place the sheep at his right hand, but the goats at the left. Then the King will say to those at his right hand, 'Come, O blessed of my Father, inherit the kingdom prepared for you from

137

the foundation of the world; for I was hungry and you gave me food, I was thirsty and you gave me drink, I was a stranger and you welcomed me, I was naked and you clothed me, I was sick and you visited me, I was in prison and you came to me.' Then the righteous will answer him 'Lord, when did we see thee hungry and feed thee, or thirsty and give thee to drink? And when did we see a stranger and welcome thee, or naked and clothe thee? And when did we see thee sick or in prison and visit thee?' And the King will answer them, 'Truly, I say to you, as you did it to one of the least of these my brethren, you did it to me.' Then he will say to those at his left hand, 'Depart from me, you cursed, into the eternal fire prepared for the devil and his angels; for I was hungry and you gave me no food, I was thirsty and you gave me no drink, I was a stranger and you did not welcome me, naked and you did not clothe me, sick and in prison and you did not visit me.' Then they also will answer, 'Lord, when did we see thee hungry or thirsty or a stranger or naked or sick or in prison, and did not minister to thee?' Then he will answer them, 'Truly, I say to you, as you did it not to one of the least of these, you did it not to me.' And they will go away into eternal punishment, but the righteous into eternal life.'' (Mt. 25,31-46).

Seen from a literary point of view, this story about the Last Judgment is part of a magnificent composition put into Christ's mouth by the evangelist, that concerns his return at the end of time (Mt. 24,1-25,46). According to this gospel, there will be war and the collapse of faith, cruelty in holy places, and every kind of misery, evil and deception (see Mt. 24,4-28).

"Immediately after the tribulation of those days the sun will be darkened, and the moon will not give its light, and the stars will fall from heaven, and the powers of

the heavens will be shaken; then will appear the sign of the Son of Man in heaven, and then all the tribes of the earth will mourn, and they will see the Son of Man coming on the clouds of heaven with power and great glory; and he will send out his angels with a loud trumpet call, and they will gather his elect from the four winds, from one end of heaven to the other" (Mt. 24,29-31).

Matthew follows this with three parables (The Faithful and Wise Servant Mt. 24,45-51; the Wise and Foolish Maidens, Mt. 25,1-13; and the Parable of the Talents, Mt. 25,14-30), that all warn us to be watchful. At the end there is the account of the second coming of the Son of Man and the Last Judgment, during which the peoples of the earth will be judged according to their deeds, and the good will be separated from the bad.

We can only understand this representation that Matthew put into Jesus's mouth if we take its literary form into account. It is neither a simile (these are always told in the present tense "What man of you, having a hundred sheep, if he has lost one of them...." Lk. 15,4), nor is it a parable (which is told in the simple past, "....There was a man who had two sons..." Lk. 15,11). The use of the future tense in the Last Judgment rather refers to the literary genre of *apocalyptic portrayal and revelations.*

The notion of the world's approaching end was common in Judaic thought from around the middle of the second century BC until the early Christian period. Correlations were seen between the future world and destiny, correlations which were expressed in the language of imagery. Consequently we are not to understand the apocalyptic biblical texts as stage directions for a production of the final drama. We must seek elsewhere for the intention of their authors. One thing is certain: the author of the Book of Revelation proclaims that through all possible misery, all conceivable tribulation, and in spite of all expected confusion and uncertainties, Jesus Christ will finally triumph. It says that God is the aim of man, the world, and the cosmos. The evangelist makes use of the images and concepts of the time known to him to depict this fulfillment and the way it will come to pass. Naturally, this does not only apply to the events immediately preceding the phenomenon of the end of time, but also to the depiction of the Last Judgment itself.

As far as the scenario is concerned, it is highly probable that it was devised by the evangelist. In the depiction of the throned Son of Man, the rabbinical concept of the "throne of magnificence" was before his eyes; according to the Talmud masters, this existed before the world was created. The judgment upon "the peoples" held by the Son of Man (who here appears as King) reminds us of the prophetic words of "the Day of Jahweh." Linked to this on the one hand, was a visible intervention in the history of Israel on Jahweh's part, with the aim of saving the chosen people and scattering their enemies (Joel 3,1-21), and on the other, the expectation of the day of judgment, from which Israel will emerge purified, and revenged upon her enemies(Mal. 3,2; Zech. 12,1-20). The *apocalyptic* concepts of "The Day of the Lord" are in accordance with the corresponding *prophetic* visions in that they express a hope for a change in the world *here on this side*; all wrongs will be put right, so that henceforth peace and justice will reign among men. Later this "Day of Judgment of Jahweh" became ever more linked to the approaching end of the world (Dan. 9,26; 12,13), the day on which — and now we have the early church interpretation — Christ will appear to pass judgment upon all peoples and nations. However, even today there is no unity among exegetes about which "peoples" the evangelist has in mind (all the Gentiles, with or without Israel? All those converted to Christianity — in other words the Christians?) One can solve the problem most convincingly if one does not solely orientate oneself towards the Old Testament concepts of Jahweh's Day (of Judgment), but rather towards Matthew's gospel. It is known that he supported the view that the end of the world would not occur before the good tidings "will be preached throughout the whole world" (Mt. 24,14). From this we may conclude that the whole of mankind is meant by the "peoples."

The image used for the judgment of the sheep would have spontaneously reminded the original listeners to Matthew's gospel of a passage from the Book of Ezekiel, "As for you, my flock, thus says the Lord God: 'Behold I judge between sheep and sheep, rams and he-goats....'" Ezek. 34,17). The separation of male from female animals arises because the latter have to be milked.[8] Naturally then, it is not the sex of the animals, but separation as such that forms the point of comparison, resulting in their being qualified as good or evil — positioned right or left of the shepherd. In fact the right side in ancient Judaism (and in the whole of the Mideast) counted as preferable, while the left was considered unlucky.

Like a shepherd who separates the sheep from the rams in the evening for milking, so at the Last Judgment the King will separate the good from the wicked. What is astonishing is that the question of Faust's Gretchen ("Now tell me, what is your stand on religion?")[9] plays absolutely no part. And what about professing Christianity? Who has received baptism? Who is affiliated to the church? We should imagine that all this belongs to the act of the Last Judgment just as much as the names of the defendants.

But instead of this, at first the talk is of eating and drinking, then of strangers and the homeless, people who cannot buy themselves clothes, and finally of the sick and the criminals.

Obviously the evangelist is here referring to the famous sermon on fasting from the book of Isaiah, in which Jahweh condemns his peoples' hypocritical sacrificial cult, and at the same time announces through the mouth of the prophet what he understands as correct fasting:

"Behold in the day of your fast you seek
your own pleasure,
and oppress all your workers.
Behold, you fast only to quarrel and
to fight
and to hit with wicked fist....
It is not this fast that I choose;
to loose the bounds of wickedness,
to undo the throngs of the yoke,
to let the oppressed go free,
and to break every yoke?
Is it not to share your bread with the hungry,
and to bring the homeless poor into your house; when
you see the naked to cover him
and not to hide yourself from your own flesh?"
Is. 58, 3f.6f)

Similar enumerations are not only found in other books of the Hebrew Bible (see Tob. 1,16-20) and in rabbinical literature, but also in the Egyptian Book of the Dead, a collection of sayings which was probably put together in the form we know in c. 1500 BC: "I have satisfied God with that which he loves. I have given bread to the hungry, water to the thirsty, clothed the naked and given the shipless a ship...".[10] It is the dead person himself who here praises his own efforts, whilst in the depiction of the Last Judgment it is the Son of Man and King (Christ is implied) who points to the merits of the good. With reference to Matthew's representation, one could say that here there is rather a reversion to old and widely spread concepts than a direct dependence upon specific literary models. However, all these historical correlations that have come down to us are only of limited interest to our problem. There is no doubt that we should pay great attention to the fact that the attainment of salvation is here dependent upon one single factor, namely on behavior towards fellow human beings, especially towards the poorest among them and that, according to the evangelist's view, it is here that our attitude towards Christ is made concrete. In this Matthew goes back to the ancient story of the King, who goes incognito through the land as a beggar, in order to test the behavior and opinions of his subjects. The statement is explicit: he who continually does a work of mercy fulfills the will of Jesus, and that is why such a work has the same worth as if one had done it unto him.

Concern for Mankind as a Way of Salvation?

The language of imagery in the Last Judgment shows that finally salvation is dependent upon faith lived, and that this living faith is manifested in "works of mercy," or as we would say today, in observing the dignity of man and in commitment to human rights.

But does not such a view almost conclude that everyone, according to his own fashion, can become blessed? And that finally — even according to the Bible

143

— the humanitarian ideal represents the real way to salvation?

However, numbers of other New Testament sayings refute this thesis, and stand diametrically opposed to such an idea, because they consider professing Christ absolutely necessary for salvation. We are reminded of the almost classic formula: "And without faith it is impossible to please him (God). For whoever would draw near to God must believe...." (Heb. 11,6). But belief is always understood in the New Testament as belief in Jesus Christ as the Son of God and the Redeemer. And this belief, according to the epistle to the Hebrews, is an imperative condition for salvation. Other witnesses to this insist that it must be sealed through baptism: "He who believes and is baptized will be saved; but he who does not believe will be condemned" (Mk. 16,16; see Acts.4,11f; Rom. 10,9f).

From this we could clearly form the impression that everyone who does not believe in Jesus Christ is excluded from salvation. But against this opinion is the fact that after being received into baptism, we are called upon to proclaim the faith, and so listen to and appropriate Jesus's message to ourselves ("Go into all the world and preach the gospel to the whole creation" Mk. 16,15). Rejection, then, only applies to those people who, although they hear and accept the good tidings, do not practice them. Both subjective and excusable motives that can lead to the rejection of the Christian message are not considered.

The New Testament expressly and repeatedly speaks of God's all-embracing will that all be saved (see Tit. 2,11; 3,4-6; 1 Tim. 4,10). If God indeed "desires all men to be saved and to come to the knowledge of the truth" (1 Tim. 2,4) their salvation can in no way be bound to church proclamation and agency, which has not reached all mankind at all times.

An application of the orthodox profession of faith to daily life is the basis of the story of the Good Samaritan and the depiction of the Last Judgment. Orthodoxy is not named as a criterion for taking possession of the kingdom (Mt. 25,34), but what is named is the right behavior towards one's fellow human beings and, before that, the subject of the Sermon on the Mount in Matthew, and in connection with the true discipleship:

"Not every one who says to me 'Lord, Lord' shall enter the kingdom of my Father who is in heaven. On that day (the Last Judgment) many will say to me 'Lord, Lord, did we not prophesy in your name, and do many mighty works in your name?' And then I will declare to them, 'I never knew you; depart from me, you evildoers'." (Mt. 7,21-23)

Mere membership in the church of Christ therefore does not guarantee salvation. There are also those "blessed of my Father" (Mt. 25,34) outside the church.

Without doubt the New Testament repeatedly underlines the significance of a proper profession of faith for man's final salvation. But on the other hand, those who through no fault of their own have not found this belief will not be excluded. The truth is that the New Testament tells us that Jesus Christ alone is the mediator between God and man (1 Tim. 2,4; Heb. 8,6; 9,14f), and that therefore also those people who do not profess him can still find salvation *through him* (see 1 Tim. 2,5-6). The door to heaven is basically open to all because Jesus's act as redeemer is for the benefit of all; that means also for those who have no knowledge of his teaching or profess the Christian belief.[11] With regard to earlier misleading teaching statements ("no salvation outside the church")[12] the Second Vatican Council has stated and interpreted its view more precisely in its Dogmatic Constitution on the Church. It is expressly taught there that God "is not distant" from those who believe otherwise, and that he does not withdraw his grace from non-believers, so that they are not exempt from salvation in so far as they seek for the truth with honest hearts, and attempt to act according to their consciences.

Finally, those who have not yet received the Gospel are related to the People of God in various ways. There is, first, that people to which the covenants and promises were made, and from which Christ was born according to the flesh (cf. Rom. 9:4-5): in view of the divine choice, they are a people most dear for the sake of the fathers, for the gifts of God are without repentance (cf. Rom. 11,28f). But the plan of salvation also includes those who acknowledge the Creator, in the first place amongst whom are the Moslems: these profess to hold the faith of Abraham, and together with us they adore the one, merciful God, mankind's judge on the last day. Nor is God remote from those who in shadows and images seek the unknown God, since he gives to all men life and breath and all things (cf. Acts 17:25-28), and since the Saviour wills all men to be saved (cf. 1 Tim. 2:4). Those who, through no fault of their own, do not know the Gospel of Christ or his Church, but who nevertheless seek God with a sincere heart, and, moved by grace, try in their actions to do his will as they know it through the dictates of their conscience — those too may achieve eternal salvation.[13]

Here we have a theological explanation of what is represented by narrative in the imagery of the Last Judgment. In contrast, however, to the Egyptian Book of the Dead, where the dead person boasts of his good deeds before the godhead in order to achieve the best

possible judgment, in Matthew the kingly judge emphasizes that all the deeds of those gathered before him
were done personally to him. Matthew here underlines
two facts; that Jesus is indeed the bringer of salvation,
and that this salvation is dependent upon how a person
(consciously or unconsciously) behaves towards Jesus
Christ. The author of the Acts of the Apostles formulates the situation both precisely and forcefully: "And
there is salvation in no one else" (Acts. 4,12).

Under the Silver Lamps

In his representation of the Last Judgment the evangelist reminds his readers that it is up to them to decide
for Jesus Christ, and thereby for or against their own
salvation — and that the decisive criterion is love for
one's fellow human beings.

Matthew's depiction of the end of time and the Last
Judgment is not to be understood as a detailed description of coming events. But because the apocalyptic
image and revelation have become extremely foreign to
us, I have attempted to translate them into our time and
our conceptual world.

I proceed from the fact that during our lives each
one of us stands in a personal and a social network of
relationships. We are shaped by the world around us,
and for our part, we influence it. All our relationships
to others, to society, to history and to the world stand,
for their part, in relationship to God. Whenever we die
and enter God's eternity, each one of us takes a piece
of the history of relationships and of the world with us,
that we have to answer for before God. And so with
the death of each individual the history of mankind as
a whole goes towards God in a gradual process. Theo-

logically, there is nothing to stop us from interpreting this *whole process* as the Last Judgment.

The whole history of mankind will come just once to fulfillment. Matthew means only this when he speaks of the second coming of the Lord, of the Last Judgment, and of the completion of creation. He does not want to fill us with fear and terror, but to show us that we are often much closer to God than we ourselves can know. It is this knowledge that lies at the basis of Tolstoy's legend. Elisyei's view is obscured and his sight poor; he imagines himself to be in a miserable peasants' hut while in reality he is already in the middle of the heavenly city of Jerusalem, directly under the silver lamps where the divine fire burns.

7
To Gain the Whole World and Lose One's Life?

Certainly one of the most widely spread diseases of our century is boredom, and linked to it, world weariness. As a rule literature is a dependable seismograph of the "Zeitgeist," and in contemporary literature its documentation is almost frightening. Plays like Samuel Beckett's "Waiting for Godot" or "End Game," novels like Jean Paul Sartre's "La Nausée" or Françoise Sagan's "Bonjour Tristesse" are regarded with an extraordinary degree of respect, because many of us contemporaries can identify ourselves closely with the persons and situations represented.

In this connection Alberto Moravia's novel "La Noia" deserves particular mention. The main character is the thirty-five-year-old painter Dino. His relationship to his mother, an ageing and wealthy widow, is troubled. "As I knew, my mother believed in nothing but money. But it is known that she sticks to 'propriety,' and amongst other things this leads to her describing herself as 'practicing' and treating all religious matters with respect."[1] One day Dino meets the seventeen-year-old Cecilia, a girl who lives from day to day, half-child, half-femme fatale. When Dino later attempts suicide, it has less to do with this problematic relationship than with the fact that in spite of this affair he is unable to find any point in life. His whole feeling for existence can be summed up in the title Moravia chose for his book: *Noia*, which means boredom. Dino says of himself:

"Nothing that I did pleased me or seemed worthwhile doing. On the other hand I couldn't imagine anything that would bring me pleasure anymore, that means anything that could have occupied me for any length of time. I did nothing, except go into my studio and leave it again with some sort of useless pretext, so that I didn't have to stay there. I bought cigarettes that I didn't even need, drank coffee that I didn't even want, bought a paper that didn't even interest me, went to a picture exhibition that didn't arouse my curiosity at all — and so on."

Dino only takes this state of affairs into account after his suicide attempt. Looking back (the whole novel is told in the first person), he realizes at the same time that boredom is as much a part of Cecilia's life as breathing.

Dino's mother suffers from the same sickness; she spends her days administering her property, receiving guests, going to the theater, while she often admits to her son that her main concern "is to kill time."

One has a tendency to see these figures in the novel as caricatures. But they are drawn from life. Moravia's protagonists verge on the monstrous. Although they achieve nothing, they could achieve everything; in spite of this (or because of it) they are bored to tears by everything. They do not feel the slightest sympathy for any one or any thing: they vegetate in a stifling way (on the very first page Dino tells us that he lies apathetically on his divan for hours at a time, staring at the ceiling); they know neither joy nor sorrow, nor any human feelings. Their whole life is a prolonged death-watch, an agony in slow motion; they literally bore themselves to death.

The Poor Rich Man and Rich Lazarus

Jesus must have been thinking of a similar situation when he told his people the parable of the moody children.

"But to what shall I compare this generation? It is like children sitting in the market places and calling to their playmates, 'We piped to you and you did not dance; we wailed and you did not mourn.'

For John came neither eating nor drinking, and they say 'He has a demon'; the Son of Man came eating and drinking, and they say 'Behold a glutton and a drunkard, a friend of tax collectors and sinners!' Yet wisdom is justified by her deeds." (Mt. 11,16-19; see Lk. 7,31-35).

Here Jesus is preaching against Israel's leading citizens who were increasingly distancing themselves from him. He compares them to a crowd of children who are bored and cannot decide on anything. Some invite their comrades to play at weddings and funerals. But the latter have no desire to perform the dance of death or the wedding roundelay. They are spoil sports, and so prevent anything from happening. In short, they prefer lolling around.

In his contrast to the choice of games, Jesus alludes to his own appearance and that of John the Baptist. John's preaching on repentance and judgment (burial) is just as much rejected as Jesus's turning towards sinners (weddings). John fasts and is considered possessed; Jesus shares meals with the despised and the outcasts, and is dubbed a "glutton and a drunkard."

151

In fact one can never do the right thing for a majority of people. There are moaners who always look on the black side of things or feel put out about something. They constantly find something to quibble about. And if they can't find something then they are morose because there is nothing for them to carp at. Basically they have no idea what they really want. They are never content because they are bored. Or the other way round; they are bored because they are never content. And if you leave them alone they are quite hurt.

Such people live from day to day, but pass life by. Jesus explains just how fatal such an attitude is in one of his parables.

"There was a rich man, who was clothed in purple and fine linen, and who feasted sumptuously every day. And at his gate lay a poor man named Lazarus, full of sores, who desired to be fed with what fell from the rich man's table; moreover the dogs came and licked his sores. The poor man died and was carried by the angels to Abraham's bosom. The rich man also died and was buried; and in Hades being in torment, he lifted up his eyes, and saw Abraham far off and Lazarus in his bosom. And he called out, 'Father Abraham, have mercy upon me, and send Lazarus to dip the end of his finger in water and cool my tongue; for I am in anguish in this flame.' But Abraham said, 'Son, remember that you in your lifetime received your good things, and Lazarus in like manner evil things; but now he is comforted here, and you are in anguish. And besides all this, between us and you a great chasm has been fixed, in order that those who would pass from here to you may not be able, and none may cross from there to us.' And he said, 'Then I beg you, father, to send him to my father's house, for I have five brothers, so that he may warn them, lest they also come into this place of torment.' But Abraham said

'They have Moses and the prophets; let them hear them.' And he said 'No, father Abraham; but if some one goes to them from the dead, they will repent.' He said to him, 'If they do not hear Moses and the prophets, neither will they be convinced if some one should rise from the dead.'" (Lk. 16,19-31).

The beginning of the story ("There was a rich man....) points to its origins; it was an Egyptian fairy story that was brought to Palestine by Jews from Alexandria. It tells of a journey into the underworld, and ends with the caution: "He who is good on this earth shall also be well treated in the realm of the dead, but he who is evil on earth will be treated evilly (there)."[2] The popular story in Palestine of the poor scholar of the law and the rich tax collector Bar Ma'jan originated from this former tale, and was soon included in the Palestinian Talmud. After the pious scholar dies he is buried quietly, while a magnificent funeral is planned for the tax collector. Just before his death the latter organizes a feast for the councilors. When they do not appear at short notice he invites the poor of the city. The reward for this good deed is the lavish funeral. The poor scholar who has led a god-fearing life receives his permanent reward in the life beyond.

Certainly Jesus must have known this story. We can suppose that it was the introduction (the invitation to the worthy councilors) that inspired him to tell the parable of the great feast (see Mt. 22,1-10; Lk. 14,16-24). However in the parable of the rich man and the beggar Lazarus, he focuses on the conclusion to the popular tale of the people. This is about just reward and deserved punishment which will be the lot of us all one day. In contrast Jesus puts the emphasis elsewhere, although reward and punishment are also the theme. Lazarus receives his share of the heavenly feast. The

153

idea for this which goes back to Isaiah (25,6) was widely known in Judaism at Jesus's time (see Mt. 8,11). The rich man, on the other hand, is cast out into the "underworld" after death, and suffers inconceivable torture, which in turn corresponds to the then current concept of life after death. To his plea to grant him some relief, Abraham replies, "Son, remember that you in your lifetime received your good things, and Lazarus in like manner evil things; but now he is comforted here, and you are in anguish" (Lk. 16,25). Is this finally the longed-for coup d'état? Does earthly well-being necessarily lead to hellish pain? Temporary misery to heavenly joy in every case? Can the hungry at last fill their stomachs and the rich go to the devil, where the poor wished them during their lifetime? Such interpretations may well spring from human wishful thinking — we say justice and mean revenge — but there is no indication of these in the text. It only seems that this parable aims in the same direction as the popular fairy story upon which it is based. In reality it presents quite a different theme. Lazarus is not "comforted" because he is miserable and covered in festering sores, and because he really has gone to the dogs (as the text expressly says, see 16,21). Rather he is saved because he has held true to God in spite of his sufferings. This is implied by the rich man's anonymity (this applies to other characters active in all Jesus's parables), whereas Lazarus is called by *name*. There is a reason for this. Lazarus (in Hebrew, Eleazar) means "he whom God helps." The name therefore demonstrates that this New Testament Job puts all his hope in God. And he who trusts in God and allows himself to be helped by him attains salvation.

It is not because of his poverty but because of his faith that Lazarus is saved. It follows then, that it is not because of his riches, but only because of his way of life or, better said, because of his life style, that the rich man is cast out. This emerges from the context within which this story is told. Jesus indicates to his listeners that they have to decide between "God and mammon" (Lk. 16,13). The evangelist comments "The Pharisees, who were lovers of money heard all this, and they scoffed at him" (Lk. 16,14). Jesus admonishes them that "what is exalted among men is an abomination in the sight of God" (Lk. 16,15), and finishes by telling them the parable of the rich man and Lazarus.

What concerns him can be found in the astonishing turn that the story finally takes. If there can be no relief given to the rich man himself, at least he would like his five brothers to be protected from a similar lot. Lazarus must warn them "lest they also come into this place of torment" (16,28). But Abraham objects that even the bodily return of someone dead could not be relied upon to change their minds and therefore their lives, for they too have not listened to Moses and the prophets.

In this statement Jesus expresses his own disappointment that his mission (which is always based upon the law — that is, upon Moses and the prophets) is widely rejected, and that no one has any belief in his signs (see Jn. 12,37). Typically enough, it is nearly always the leaders of society (by that I mean the wealthy) who are distant from Jesus. This experience is also expressed in the parable of the rich man and Lazarus. If we are talking about *life*, riches easily become a trap. And if this trap snaps to, the whole being and effort of a person only aims at increasing possessions, at gaining power, at enjoying life. Such a one is deaf to the voice of the heart and blind to the poor in front of the door.

"Repent a Day before Death"

In his warning against a superficial life Jesus was not alone in the Judaism of the time. Rabbi Eleazar, a Talmud master of the first century reports that he has called upon the people to repent a day before their death.

"His pupils asked Rabbi Eleazar; 'Does man then know upon which day he will die?' And he answered them, 'No. Therefore there is all the more reason that he should today do penitence, in case he dies tomorrow. And so he will find himself repenting throughout life.'"[3]

This thought returns again, both in Jesus's preaching and in some of his parables. Whenever he castigates superficiality at the same time he calls us to vigilance and readiness to repent and change our lives.

"But know this, that if the householder had known in what part of the night the thief was coming, he would have watched and would not have let his house be broken into. Therefore you also must be ready, for the Son of Man is coming at an hour you do not expect" (Mt. 24,43f; compare Lk. 12,39f).

It is possible that Jesus is here alluding to a recent burglary still fresh in the minds of his listeners. The incident contains a lesson for life; do not behave in the same careless way as the thoughtless householder when your life is at stake! Keep your eyes and your ears open, and above all, open your hearts!

This situation presents itself in the parable of the guest without the right clothes (which can actually only be understood within the context of the rabbinical literature of the time).

"But when the king came in to look at the guests, he saw there was a man who had no wedding garment, and he said to him, 'Friend, how did you get in here without a wedding garment?' And he was speechless. Then the king said to the attendants, 'Bind him hand and foot, and cast him into the outer darkness; there men will weep and gnash their teeth. For many are called, but few are chosen'." (Mt. 22,11-14).

Matthew tells this story immediately after his version of the parable of the royal marriage feast (see 22,1-10)[4] to which the king invites those from the highways, after the original guests have refused.

At first we are naturally tempted to excuse the man. Is it not expressly said that the servants have taken the guests off the streets? How can it then be explained that the other guests present themselves in festive garb? Some interpreters of the parable assume that the king himself has provided suitable clothes for his guests with the invitation. However, this explanation fails. The custom of giving those invited a festive garment at the entrance (or in an anteroom) is not found anywhere. In interpreting this story, we must simply proceed from the fact that all the remaining guests have got themselves correctly dressed; and that the king is at first surprised at, but in no way annoyed about, the one man who has apparently thumbed his nose at good taste and propriety. This can be seen from his words; *"Friend, how did you get in here without a wedding garment?"* The man does not know how to reply. In other words, it is entirely his own fault, and he can't find any excuse. The narrator presupposes that he too had the chance to dress according to the custom.

Only Matthew links the episode of the guest without wedding dress and the parable of the royal wedding feast. Originally however, it was passed down inde-

157

pendently of the parable. We too cannot overlook the reference to the early Christian community. It allows us to come to the conclusion that among the "invited" (interpreting the imagery, among the newly baptized) there were already obvious signs of lukewarmness and indifference. In linking the episode of the guest without a wedding garb to the parable of the royal wedding feast, the evangelist reminds us that indifference to the good tidings will be condemned by the "king."

This episode probably had its origin in a Talmudic story.

"A King invited his subjects to a feast, without fixing a definite time for this. The clever ones adorned themselves, and sat at the entrance to the palace. They thought: 'There is nothing lacking in the King's residence.' The stupid ones went about their work. They thought: 'Can there be a feast without preparation?'

Suddenly the King bade his subjects to come to table. The clever ones appeared well adorned before him, the stupid ones appeared in dirty garments. The King rejoiced over his clever subjects, and was angry about the stupid ones. He said: 'Those who have adorned themselves for the feast shall sit, eat and drink. But those who have not adorned themselves shall stand and watch.'" [5]

The Talmud attributes this story to a certain Rabbi Joachanan, who was teaching about 80 AD. But probably the story was told in a similar form at Jesus's time. It is only when we compare both stories that it becomes clear why the man without a wedding garment is so harshly treated. It is because of his easygoing attitude. Like the rich man he has misjudged the seriousness of the situation; he has totally underestimated his position. In his thoughtlessness he does not grasp the fact that there are moments that one may not miss at any cost, because the whole of life, all the future, even one's whole happiness hangs upon them.

Jesus knew that such a moment presented itself when he spoke to his fellow countrymen. "The time is fulfilled, and the kingdom of God is at hand; repent, and believe in the gospel" (Mk. 1.15). This call blared like a fanfare of trumpets. Generations of pious Jews had dreamt of this kingdom of God, and spoken about it — and were used to this kind of talk. Suddenly there is someone there who discerns with all certainty that God's kingdom has become visible within him: "But if it is by the spirit of God that I cast out demons, then the kingdom of God has come upon you" (Mt. 12,28). No one who knew how to interpret the signs of the times could avoid this:

"From the fig tree learn a lesson: as soon as its branch becomes tender and puts forth its leaves, you know that summer is near. So also, when you see these things taking place, (the previously described events of the end of time; see Mk. 13,24-27) you know that he is near, at the very gates" (Mk. 13,28f; compare Mt. 24,32f;Lk. 21,29-31).

Although Jesus names no special time, he is yet firmly convinced that the completion of God's rule, and with it the arrival of the Son of Man, are imminent: "Truly, I say to you, this generation will not pass away before all these things take place" (Mk. 13,30; compare 9,1; Mt. 10,23).

Even if we understand by "generation" not merely people living now but a whole age, the parousia (the theological term for the arrival of the Lord) of Jesus has not been fulfilled. Did Jesus therefore make a mistake?

At first sight this question might appear heretical. But this impression rests upon the assumption that of necessity omniscience belongs to Jesus's divinity. But the idea of Jesus as God "dressed up" as man is far more heretical. At the basis of this lies the silent assumption that a limited knowledge represents a lack that is incompatible with the divine perfection attributed to Jesus. It is precisely this assumption that needs correcting. The readiness to learn and growth of knowledge belong essentially to the process of human development.

Every human being realizes himself in dialogue and in relationship to others; he finds his identity first of all in confrontation with himself and his surroundings. Applied to Jesus this means that one can distinguish between his human knowledge and his divine consciousness as Messiah, but may not separate these two from each other. With increasing age, Jesus gradually broadened himself in human (profane and religious) experience of knowledge. At the same time by degrees his messianic consciousness of the Son, that is, the certainty of being the promised redeemer, also gained sharper contours. Within his human development which included a process of learning, he became ever increasingly aware of his messianic mission. In a word: Jesus discovered himself to be the Son of God in a human way, and this within processes of experience and knowledge which stretched from his youth to his death on the cross. In no way does Jesus's consciousness as the Messiah require the assumption that he had a part of the divine omniscience. He emphasizes expressly that neither he nor "even the angels in heaven, nor the Son, but only the Father" knows of that day or that hour (Mk. 13, 32 par). Indeed, Jesus was *convinced* that his generation would experience the coming of the Son of Man.

Was Jesus then mistaken in his expectation? The question demands a differentiated reply. It was only natural for Jesus to believe that "the day of the Lord" (Amos 5,18; Zeph. 1, 14ff) — the day which Jews of that time believed to be the day of God's judgment on the world — was immediately ahead. In so far as this prediction has not been fulfilled, one does in fact have to speak of a mistaken assumption. But we should remember at the same time that Jesus's mistake in no way touches his message. His *immediate* expectation simply forms the framework or the concrete requirement within which he proclaims his message of the arrival of God's kingdom, and calls his people to repent. That the parousia of Jesus is not fulfilled does not speak against the truth of his preaching, which *finally* does not aim at announcing the approaching end, but at bringing mankind to its senses and to repentance.

Jesus himself did not experience the end of the world he had expected. But the early Christian community remained convinced that they would not have to wait long for God's judgment, which was linked to the second coming of Christ. There is no doubt that this emerges in the first epistle to the Thessalonians, which Paul probably wrote during the winter of 50-51 AD in Corinth (it is the oldest of all extant New Testament manuscripts). In it the apostle expresses the hope that he will experience the second coming himself (see 1 Thess. 4,15-18).

Because the parousia of the early community was not fulfilled, the evangelists saw themselves forced to demand even more insistent vigilance from the Christian community.

The same warning not to fix one's life upon the second best but to stay watchful is contained in the parable of the ten bridesmaids. Typically there is talk of a feast at the end.

"Then the kingdom of heaven shall be compared to ten maidens who took their lamps and went to meet the bridegroom. Five of them were foolish, and five were wise. For when the foolish took their lamps, they took no oil with them; but the wise took flasks of oil with their lamps. As the bridegroom was delayed, they all slumbered and slept. But at midnight there was a cry 'Behold, the bridegroom! Come out to meet him.' Then all those maidens rose and trimmed their lamps. And the foolish said to the wise, 'Give us some of your oil, for our lamps are going out.' But the wise replied, 'Perhaps there will not be enough for us and for you; go rather to the dealers and buy for yourselves.' And while they went to buy, the bridegroom came, and those who were ready went in with him to the marriage feast; and the door was shut. Afterward the other maidens came also, saying 'Lord, lord, open to us.' But he replied, 'Truly, I say to you, I do not know you.'" (Mt. 25,1-12).

To begin with, this parable makes us feel that the confusion ruling at this marriage has also found expression in the story telling. First of all, it is incomprehensible why the bridegroom makes everyone wait for him. Isn't it always men who constantly reproach women that they are never ready when they are dressing, putting on their finery and make up? Besides, the narrator has no word for the bride; it is almost as if she isn't there. And how can one explain that five of the bridesmaids send their companions to the dealers in the middle of the night? Do we not have an impression of just a little jealousy, or malicious joy on the quiet, or even spite?

Most of these questions are unnecessary if we remember that we are here dealing with a Mideastern village. The bridesmaids have gathered together in the bride's house with her relations and friends. They are all waiting for the bridegroom who must take his bride home. The wedding should take place in his house around evening. But no one is surprised that he arrives late; on the contrary! They would all have been astonished if he had *not* come late. And of course they all know that he is already quite near at hand, presumably in a house that belongs to the bride's relations. According to traditional Mideastern custom, these are haggling for the last time over the final sum that the man's family will have to pay on his death or if he should divorce his wife. It is an honor for the bride if these discussions go on for a long time; her relations then show how unwilling they are to part with her. When the messengers come at midnight to tell the closest relations that everything has been arranged and that the bridegroom is coming, a few of the bridesmaids notice that their lamps are going out. While they are buying oil from the dealer (not at all difficult; the whole village is on its feet), their companions accompany the pair and the wedding party to the house of the bridegroom, where the wedding will take place, followed by the feast.

We could have a good laugh about these five bridesmaids who first of all have no light and are then left standing, were it not for the extremely hard ending which shows that we are not simply dealing with an anecdote, but with a serious warning.

"Lord, lord, open to us!" This cry from the bridesmaids points to other words from Jesus in Matthew's gospel; "Not everyone who says to me 'Lord, lord' shall enter the kingdom of heaven, but he who does the will of my Father, who is in heaven" (Mt. 7,21). In the bridegroom's answer "I do not know you" we are dealing with a rabbinical disownment formula that points to a legal situation. In fact the final scene does contain a judgment of the five foolish bridesmaids. There lies the main accent of the whole story, as it is expressed in the final comment "Watch therefore, for you know neither the day nor the hour" (Mt. 25,13).

We can no longer reconstruct how Jesus told this parable. But certainly he related it to the end of the world that he was expecting. On the other hand, the evangelist turns it allegorically towards the situation of the early Christian community living in expectation of the second coming. Christ himself is the bridegroom. The ten bridesmaids symbolize the baptized. Some of them begin to adapt to the long delay, aware that they must *always* be ready. Others behave foolishly and thoughtlessly. They are tired of waiting and relax their zealous faith. They are no longer on their guard, and therefore risk salvation.

"Be watchful!"

The same situation is reflected in two other parables, the first of them about a doorkeeper.

"Take heed, watch; for you do not know when the time will come. It is like a man going on a journey, when he leaves home and puts his servants in charge, each with his work, and commands the doorkeeper to be on the watch. Watch therefore — for you do not know when the master of the house will come, in the evening, or at midnight, or at cockcrow, or in the morning — lest he come suddenly and find you asleep. And what I say to you (Peter, James, John and Andrew; see Mk. 13,3) I say to all: Watch" (Mk. 13,33-37).

The man who has set off on a journey represents the risen and ascended Christ. Each within the circle of

164

domestic servants — here the Christian community is implied — has a special duty to fulfill. The doorkeeper has a particularly important function; from his position he will be the first to see the homeward-bound master, and this refers to the second coming of Christ. But the warning that he should fulfill his task responsibly does not only apply to him but to the whole domestic staff, that is, to all the baptized who must reckon with the return of the master at any time, that is, with the second coming. The more the parousia is delayed, the greater the danger that enthusiasm will flag.

This thought is also the basis of the second parable that tells of a servant who is put to the test by his master.

"Who then is the faithful and wise servant, whom his master has set over his household, to give them their food at the proper time? Blessed is that servant whom his master when he comes will find so doing. Truly, I say to you, he will set him over all his possessions: But if that wicked servant says to himself, 'My master is delayed,' and begins to beat his fellow servants, and eats and drinks with the drunken, the master of that servant will come on a day when he does not expect him and at an hour he does not know, and will punish him and put him with the hypocrites; there men will weep and gnash their teeth" (Mt. 24,45-51; see Lk. 12,42-46).

In the German version of the ecumenical translation of the New Testament this parable has the title "Of the faithful and unfaithful servant." But we are only speaking of *one* servant (or slave, which amounts to the same thing). He has been appointed representative of his master during the latter's absence, thereby becoming superior to the domestic staff and the remaining farm hands. His new position as head servant involves greater responsibility. At the same time it gives him a feeling of freedom that he has not known before; his

165

tongue is loosened, he has the last word. And because his master allows himself and the servant time, he has the choice between behaving like a cad and a blackguard, or doing his duty and carrying out his responsibilities.

It seems reasonable to suppose that in this parable Jesus wants to remind the leaders of Israel of their responsibility. The evangelists make a warning out of it for the heads of the Christian community. These represent the absent (ascended) "Lord" until the day of his second coming which no one knows. They carry particular responsibility for all the people in the house; and more than the others, they are tempted to dismiss all thought of the master's return (we are reminded somewhat of Dostoevski's Inquisitor!), and to put their own interests first. They are confronted with the danger of losing their positions and begin to bully their fellow servants. In short, they are the ones who ingratiate themselves by carousing with their chums instead of giving the other servants food; or one could say indulging in their own pleasures instead of sharing out the bread of life.

The punishment threatened for the head servant's possible failure naturally seems disproportionately severe [tr. note: the master "shall cut him asunder" — the King James's version and the current German ecumenical version]. We should remember here that extremely cruel treatment to slaves in the ancient world was the order of the day; we find examples of men being chopped into pieces not only in secular literature but in the Bible itself (1 Sam. 15,33; Dan. 2,5). Moreover we can only do justice to the fearful threats of the master if we translate the imagery literally. The measure of the punishment threatened informs us of the actual scope

166

of the responsibility; the more all embracing this is, the more intensely it must be observed.

We may assume that in this parable the evangelists are not simply telling us that holders of high office sometimes stumble, but that they are also alluding to abuses that took place within church organization. And indeed it occurs again and again that some servants in the church prefer to come forward as princes of the church; that the guardians of faith behave like judges of the faithful, particularly in matters of morals, and that the shepherds only spend time with their sheep when they can shear them in peace and quiet and no wolf appears over the horizon.

If in the parable the master of the servant abusing his office threatens with extreme sanctions, his warning does not spring from any kind of craving for revenge; it is merely that such reprehensible behavior has to be denounced.

The parables on vigilance are particularly good examples that the evangelists do not simply hand down most of the stories Jesus told but relate them vividly to the concrete situation of the Christian community at the time. While Jesus was thinking of "the day of the Lord" when he told these stories, they are newly interpreted and at the same time re-worked by the evangelists to accord with expectation of the second coming of Christ.

That the delay of the parousia created problems insistently demanding a solution can be seen clearly in late New Testament writings. Thus with regard to these questions the anonymous author of the second epistle of Peter which appeared during the first half of the second century (2 Pet. 3,3-4) points to Psalm 90, when he says "....with the Lord one day is as a thousand years, and a thousand years as one day. The Lord is not slow about his promise as some count slowness, but is

167

forbearing toward you, not wishing that any should perish, but that all should reach repentance. But the day of the Lord will come like a thief...." (2 Pet. 3,8-10; see Ps. 90,4).

The early church had difficulty in thinking of the second coming in the far distant future. But it was just such a consideration which eventually convinced the church of the earlier centuries that the concern should be with the symbolic and not with the strictly literal New Testament pronouncements on the parousia of Christ; we get the implied point if we can speak of *the meeting with Christ* that ensues at one's death rather than of a second coming of Christ. Then the account spoken of in the parables on watchfulness, generally depicted as judgment, will be demanded of each person.

If we read and interpret these parables today from this background, now as before their basic message remains valid. They warn us not to replace God with idols. They remind us that we should take life seriously and not lose ourselves in non-commitment. Their basic message can be formulated in one sentence: live so that you can stand firm to yourselves; then you will also stand firm before God.

8

Jesus, a Poor Man, Speaks about Money

"Man shall not live by bread alone, but by every word that proceeds from the mouth of God" (Mt. 4,4). This proverbial way of talking goes back to the Hebrew Bible (Deut. 8,3) and seems even at the time of Jesus to have been one of those insights that one neither takes seriously nor questions, but rather tries to avoid. However Jesus reminds us in a parable that by doing so one can put one's whole life at stake.

"And he told them a parable, saying, 'The land of the rich man brought forth plentifully; and he thought to himself, 'What shall I do, for I have nowhere to store my crops?' And he said 'I will do this: I will pull down my barns, and build larger ones; and there I will store all my grain and my goods. And I will say to my soul, Soul, you have ample goods laid up for many years; take your ease, eat, drink and be merry.' But God said to him, 'Fool! This night your soul is required of you; and the things you have prepared, whose will they be?''' (Lk. 12,16-20).

Luke hands down this story together with other instructions of Jesus about the correct way of dealing with earthly goods. The outward occasion, an inheritance quarrel between two brothers, is the theme the evangelist adopts (see 12,13f). But instead of simply intervening in this, Jesus gives those standing around

169

the example of a rich man whose whole life is concerned with his possessions. God's merciless speech at the end may give us the impression that Jesus wants to remind us that we must calculate the possibility of sudden death into our plans for arranging our lives. But this impression is deceptive. It would also be wrong to assume that Jesus is inviting his contemporaries to forget the future and live for the day. It also has nothing to do with whether it is better to harvest your goods carefully than to squander them carelessly. The story also contains no hidden reproach for those who make an effort to give their livelihood a secure basis.

The introduction tells us what this parable is about: "Take heed, and beware of all covetousness; for a man's life does not consist in the abundance of his possessions." (Lk. 12,15). The message is directed against those people whose moral concepts do not go beyond *material possessions* because they cannot think straight, and have nothing in their heads but money. Men particularly try to compensate for their weakness and poverty by constantly talking about their success with women or boasting about their rising careers. This may give them a moment of satisfaction, but no inner peace. There is nothing left to them but to make more conquests and more money. They have no idea that just looking at a rose can bring great joy to a person.

The story of the rich corn owner may appear edifying. But we must take notice of the tone: "You fools!" It addresses those who brag of their business ability, not noticing that they are simply exposing their limitations.

170

The Royal Child

"For what does it profit a man if he gains the whole world and loses or forfeits himself?" (Lk. 9,25) This question is found in various forms and not only in the Bible; numerous poets and thinkers have seized hold of it. One of them was the French airman and writer Antoine de Saint-Exupéry in his fairy tale "The Little Prince."[1]

In this world-famous story Saint-Exupéry confronts the world of children with the adult world. As a result of mechanical failure, an airman is forced to land his plane in the middle of the desert. The next day he is woken up by "a most extraordinary small person" who —as the airman finds out in the course of time — comes from a far distant planet, where he owns a rose with four thorns.

During his journey to earth the little prince has visited various tiny planets, on which he got to know quite a lot of grown ups: a senile king, who is very happy about the visit because his only other subject is an old rat. On the next planet there is a conceited man, who only wears his hat so that he can greet you if you salute him. Then there is the tippler who drinks because he wants to forget that he drinks; a lamplighter whose job it is to light the lamp and then put it out. He holds strictly to these instructions although his planet turns faster and faster, so that every day and night now only last half a minute. Then comes the explorer who has never left his desk and yet thinks that he knows the whole world. Later, on the planet earth, which according to the explorer "has a good reputation," the little prince meets a railway switchman who sorts out "travellers, in bundles of a thousand," and a merchant who

171

sells pills "invented to quench thirst." You can save a great deal of time by taking them.

In the eyes of the little prince the grown ups are "very strange," "certainly altogether extraordinary," above all because they look upon their being grown up as a duty and the fulfilling of this duty as a virtue.

From the viewpoint of the little prince the whole adult world is similar to a great tragi-comedy. The king, for example, is nothing without his subject. To make the conceited man happy, the prince expresses his admiration for him. But adds: "But what is there in that to interest you so much?" But the tippler leaves him speechless. He only has regrets for the lamplighter who cannot allow himself a second's rest: if only he could at least enjoy the one thousand, four hundred and forty sunsets "with which the planet was blest" during the twenty four hours of its rapid rotation! It is totally incomprehensible to him that the explorer cannot write about his wonderful flower in his geography books simply because it is "ephemeral." And to the merchant who sells pills and proudly points out that according to the experts, his thirst quenching tablets save fifty-three minutes a week because one has no need to drink he says "....if I had fifty-three minutes to spend as I like, I should walk at my leisure toward a spring of fresh water." The narrator comments:

"Grown-ups love figures. When you tell them that you have made a new friend, they never ask you any questions about essential matters. They never say to you 'What does his voice sound like? What games does he love best? Does he collect butterflies?' Instead, they demand; 'How old is he? How many brothers has he? How much does he weigh? How much money does his father make?' Only from these figures do they think they have learned anything about him.

If you were to say to the grown-ups: 'I saw a beautiful house made of rosy brick, with geraniums in the windows and doves on the roof,' they would not be able to get any idea of the house at all. You would have to say to them: 'I saw a house that cost 4,000 pounds.' Then they would exclaim: 'Oh, what a pretty house that is!'"

To Eugen Drewermann all the grown-up figures in this fairy story are shattering "portraits of loneliness." Precisely *because* they want to be adult at any price, they are so serious and humorless, so embittered and obstinate, and above all so obsessed with property. They certainly have "news about the world"; but what they lack is "the art of life."[2]

This is most clearly expressed in the meeting of the little prince and the businessman.

"The fourth planet belonged to a businessman. This man was so much occupied that he did not even raise his head at the little prince's arrival.

'Good morning,'the little prince said to him. 'Your cigarette has gone out.'

'Three and two make five. Five and seven make twelve. Twelve and three make fifteen. Good morning. Fifteen and seven make twenty- two. Twenty-two and six make twenty-eight. I haven't time to light it again. Twenty-six and five make thirty-one. Phew! Then that makes five-hundred-and-one million, six-hundred-twenty-two thousand, seven-hundred-thirty one.'

'Five hundred million what?' asked the little prince.

'Eh? Are you still there?'...

'Millions of those little objects,' he said, 'which one sometimes sees in the sky.'

'Flies?'

'Oh, no. Little glittering objects.'

'Bees?'

'Oh, no. Little golden objects that set lazy men to idle dreaming. As for me, I am concerned with matters of consequence. There is no time for idle dreaming in my life.'

'Ah! You mean the stars?'

'Yes, that's it. The stars.'

'And what do you do with five-hundred millions of stars?'

'Five-hundred-and-one million, six-hundred-twenty-two thousand, seven-hundred-thirty-one. I am concerned with matters of consequence: I am accurate.'

'And what do you do with these stars?'

'What do I do with them?'

'Yes.'

'Nothing. I own them.'

'You own the stars?'

'Yes'...

'And what good does it do you to own the stars?'

'It does me the good of making me rich.'

'And what good does it do you to be rich?'

'It makes it possible for me to buy more stars, if any are discovered.'...

'How is it possible for one to own the stars?'

'To whom do they belong?' the businessman retorted, peevishly.

'I don't know. To nobody.'

'Then they belong to me, because I was the first person to think of it.'

'Is that all that is necessary?'

'Certainly. When you find a diamond that belongs to nobody, it is yours. When you discover an island that belongs to nobody, it is yours. When you get an idea before anyone else, you take out a patent on it: it is yours. So with me: I own the stars, because nobody else before me ever thought of owning them.'

'Yes, that is true,' said the little prince. 'And what do you do with them?'

'I administer them,' replied the businessman. 'I count them and recount them. It is difficult. But I am a man who is naturally interested in matters of consequence.'

The little prince was still not satisfied.

'If I owned a silk scarf,' he said, 'I could put it around my neck and take it away with me. If I owned a flower, I could pluck that flower and take it away with me. But you cannot pluck the stars from heaven.....'

'No. But I can put them in the bank.'

'Whatever does that mean?'

'That means that I write the number of my stars on a little paper. And then I put this paper in a drawer and lock it with a key.'

'And that is all?'

'That is enough,' said the businessman.

'It is entertaining,' thought the little prince. 'It is rather poetic. But it is of no great consequence.'

On matters of consequence, the little prince had ideas which were very different from those of the grown-ups.

'I myself own a flower,' he continued his conversation with the businessman, 'which I water every day. I own three volcanoes, which I clean out every week (for I also clean out the one that is extinct; one never knows). It is of some use to my volcanoes, and it is of some use to

175

my flower, that I own them. But you are of no use to the stars.....'

The businessman opened his mouth, but he found nothing to say in answer. And the little prince went away.

'The grown-ups are certainly altogether extraordinary' he said simply, talking to himself as he continued on his journey.

Basically "The Little Prince" concerns itself solely with the isolation of man, with his inability to be himself and to *live*, and with his need to oversee everything, and so have everything under his control — and this only succeeds to the extent that he has power and possessions at his disposal. But he who makes his life dependent upon these things lives in continual fear of somehow or somewhere getting a raw deal.

Rushing around department stores, climbing up the ladder of success, holding the reins of power in one's hands; does not this whole parlor game amount to a *hell of enjoyment?*

Naturally others must suffer the results, because if only career and bank account are important, it inevitably leads to one no longer regarding one's fellow human beings as people, but as objects. One then only speaks of units of force, units of competition, work units. The individual has no leisure time, he is administered, objectified. His needs and his abilities are only interesting in so far as they can further a business, a group, or a single ruler. And those who can no longer keep pace with the processes of production or achievement do not count any more; the old, the sick, the handicapped are seen as a burden.

Wherever *to have* has priority over *to be*, people tread upon each other and die the terrible death from bread alone.

Obviously "grown-ups love figures" because they *are* convinced that they only are what they *have*. According to Erich Fromm, such an enslavement necessarily leads to loss of identity:

"In the mode of having there is no living relationship between that which I have and myself. It and I have become things, and I have it because I have the chance to appropriate it to myself. But the opposite relationship exists: it has me, for my feeling of identity, or my psychic health are dependent upon having it (and as many other things as possible). The mode of having....makes subject and object into things......Most people do not know that they can only begin to use their own abilities and to go forward under their own strength when they have thrown away the crutches of possessions. What holds them back is the illusion that they cannot go forward alone, and would break down if they were not supported by their possessions."[3]

Erich Fromm's conclusion sounds like an exegetical commentary on the parable of the rich corn owner.

"The Little Prince," which to a certain extent personifies Fromm's thinking, shows what the logic of "the grown-ups" makes out of people: sad figures, clowns, figures of fun, or just weaklings — actually *fools*, as Jesus says in his parable.

In contrast to Erich Fromm and Antoine de Saint-Exupéry, the Bible does not only draw upon the human treasure of experience, but over and above that, passes on a religious message.

This aspect is not mentioned in Saint-Exupéry, although in his figure of the little prince he goes back to the religious *world of imagery*, more closely to the theme of the royal child who descends to our world and teaches mankind to see everything through different eyes. Certainly the figure of the little prince arouses our longing for something quite different. But his appearance is like a dream. There is no place for such a person in our world; as he himself says to the airman, it draws him back to his star: "You will suffer. I shall look as if I were dead; and that will not be true.....You understand...it is too far. I cannot carry this body with me. It is too heavy."

Without doubt the little prince proclaims a message for humanity, in so far as he gives us courage not to allow our dreams to be destroyed, and to view the world through the innocent eyes of a child. But he feels himself to be a stranger among the adults; nothing holds him to a world in which people are all oriented towards material success and are therefore enslaved. Such a condition brings no *redemption* but leaves a residue of melancholy and sadness.

In contrast to the little prince, Jesus does not confine himself to establishing that "the grown-ups" are strange: and he never considers withdrawing from this world: he proposes quite different alternatives. Naturally he presents them in the form of a parable.

What Is Necessary

"The kingdom of heaven is like a treasure hidden in a field, which a man found and covered up; then in his joy he goes and sells all that he has and buys that field.
Again, the kingdom of heaven is like a merchant in search of fine pearls, who on finding one pearl of great value, went and sold all that he had and bought it." (Mt. 13, 44-46).

With his preaching of "the kingdom of heaven" Jesus wants to prevent people from siding with those who are greedy for power and possessions, and from making a pact with those in control. The kingdom that Jesus proclaims is not a playground for the princes of this world.

When Matthew speaks of "the kingdom of heaven" he is definitely not thinking of a world beyond. Contemporary rabbinical custom avoided using the name of God and replaced it with the concept of "heaven"; accordingly the kingdom of heaven signifies "the kingdom of God."

The man who finds the treasure disposes of all his wealth in order to possess what he has discovered. The fact that he does not carry away the treasure immediately is because the law of the time maintained that such a finding did not belong to the finder but to the man who owned the ground upon which it was discovered. It is the same with the merchant, whom one imagines to be a jeweller. At any price he wants to have the most precious of all pearls that has ever come to his notice.

The treasure and the pearl stand for the kingdom of God. A single sentence is able to express what this kingdom announced by Jesus consists in; it realizes itself everywhere the father or the mother of all people can be seen in God, and where our brothers or sisters can be recognized in every person, and where we know ourselves to be bound to the whole of creation in a brotherly and sisterly way. In other words, whenever we try to live in unity with God, with our fellow human beings and with nature, we will find ourselves again at the gate to the flowering garden of God's kingdom.

Both the happy finder and the lucky merchant could have found easier and completely legal ways of gaining possession of what they desired — for instance, they could have borrowed the money for the purchases. However, by pointing out that both "sold all" Jesus underlines that the gift of the kingdom of God (it is after all a treasure) is not only worth uncompromising commitment, it also *demands* it!

Of course the coded message of the kingdom of God contains not only an individual but also a social dimension. It is not merely concern for one's own salvation, but also concern for other people and for the world that is with us and around us as well, that contributes to the humanization of society, and thereby to the growth of God's kingdom.

This social aspect of the proclamation of God's kingdom is particularly emphasized by Luke. His interpretation of the parable of the great banquet is a good example of this.

"A man once gave a great banquet, and invited many; and at the time for the banquet he sent his servant to say to those who had been invited, 'Come; for all is now ready.' But they all alike began to make excuses. The first said to him, 'I have bought a field, and I must go and see it; I pray you, have me excused.' And another said, 'I have bought five yoke of oxen, and I go to examine them; I pray you, have me excused.' And another said, 'I have married a wife, and therefore I cannot come.' So the servant came and reported this to his master. Then the householder in anger said to his servant, 'Go out quickly to the streets and lanes of the city and bring in the poor and maimed and blind and lame.' And the servant said 'Sir, what you commanded has been done, and still there is room.' And the master said to the servant 'Go out to the highways and hedges, and compel people to come in, that my house may be filled. For I tell you, none of the men who were invited shall taste my banquet.'" (Lk. 14,16-24)

We know that Matthew has passed down a similar parable in which the kingdom of God is compared to a king who is preparing for his son's marriage. The servants who are to call the guests to the wedding are misused by the latter, and then killed. The king has the murderers destroyed and burns their town, and then invites everyone from the streets "both bad and good; so the wedding hall was filled with guests." (Mt. 22,2-10).

The two different versions tell us that the same story is the basis of both, but that in the course of time certain alterations occurred during the transmission.

Matthew applies the parable in an allegorical way to the situation in the early church. The king stands for God, the son for Jesus, and the wedding for the coming of the Messiah. The invitation is sent out to the people of Israel, but they do not comply with it. The destruction of the town applies to the destruction of Jerusalem, which Matthew interprets as the punishment deserved for the rejection of the Messiah. The servants symbolize Jesus's disciples, who are persecuted by their Jewish compatriots, and therefore see themselves forced to proclaim their message of Jesus, the crucified and resurrected, to the people of the "thoroughfares" (the gentiles are implied).

But how did *Jesus* tell this story and how did he understand it? This question can be answered if we pay attention to what both versions of the text have in common: a man organizes a marriage feast. Those invited stay away. The host asks all those who can be reached to come to him. The sense is clear: Jesus is the messenger who proclaims God's message. But the political leaders and religious representatives of Israel reject it. Therefore Jesus turns to those who were at the time considered cast out by God only because they were ignorant and unable to observe the instructions of the law. These are the poor, the sinners, the gentiles. God's good tidings are meant for *them*.

In contrast to Matthew (who applies the parable to the situation in the early church), Luke links a lesson on social behavior to this story. This is already clear in the introduction:

"When you give a dinner or a banquet, do not invite your friends or your brothers or your kinsmen or the rich neighbors, lest they also invite you in return, and you be repaid. But when you give a feast, invite the poor, the maimed, the lame, the blind, and you will be blessed, because they cannot repay you. You will be repaid at the resurrection of the just." (Lk. 14,12-14)

This introduction corresponds to the invitation which now goes out to "the poor, the maimed, the lame, the blind." Thus Luke forms the original parable into an example of proper behavior towards those in need.

Luke's Jesus does not want to criticize the wealthy Pharisees whose guest he is by his talk (14,1), nor is he concerned to propose the kind of dinner one should give the poor. Rather he disapproves of the behavior of those people who expect a counter obligation for every obligation, and a favor for every favor. He judges the common social practice of giving and taking, which rests upon arithmetical thinking and calculated dealing, and in this way reduces lives between people to purely business links. As long as one only has one's own advantage before one's eyes, one cannot build up any relationship with another person: one can only give him or her *something*. Only if one can overcome thinking about giving and taking, can one give something of *oneself.* To put it briefly: everything that we wish to have for ourselves separates us from the other; what we share binds us to the other.

"If you will not become as little children"

In contrast to Saint-Exupéry's little prince, who finds the grown-ups strange because he views the world through the eyes of a child, Jesus says that one must " receive the kingdom of God like a child" (Mk. 10,15), a warning that the contentious Catholic writer Georges Bernanos sounds in his famous "Sermon of an Atheist on the Feast of the little Saint Thérèse of Lisieux" in which someone who denies God calls to his Christian fellow citizens:

"So become like a child, flee into childhood that rescues you. If the powerful in this world ask you awkward questions about a number of precarious topics: about modern war, about sticking to contracts, about capitalism, do not be ashamed to reply that you are stupid, that the gospel will answer for you. Perhaps then the word of God will work miracles, and the people of good will for whom it was spoken, will gather together." [4]

Christianity has always known theoretically that the measuring scales of the gospel are not balanced according to the standards of the world — and in practice, forgotten this again and again. Of course Jesus neither glorified misery nor celebrated poverty. He invites his people to become like children, to protect themselves from the greed for possessions, and to turn towards the poor and the least of his people, because he wants to protect us from losing ourselves.

Sometimes this message is proclaimed from thrones and from palaces, and this is more than embarrassing. The poor wandering poet from Galilee had no social ambitions for himself. The social position of a person did not count for him — what counted was the right attitude towards one's fellow human beings. And this is also expressed in the way in which we handle earthly goods.

9
Decisions for Life?

Sometimes we have to make decisions that are binding for the rest of our lives. During a church marriage the bridal pair are asked whether they are willing to stand by each other through both good and bad times "until death us do part." When members of an order profess their vows, they promise to observe these faithfully until the end of their lives. And yet marriages are often broken after a short time, and people in orders leave their spiritual communities to resume a place in secular society.

To a certain extent, lifetime decisions are never made just once. If a nun says at her silver jubilee that she will continue to observe the evangelical counsel and serve God and man within her community — and this in spite of all past failures — she is not only repeating an earlier decision, but at the same time making a new one.

This means that once we have made decisions for life, we cannot simply rest upon them. We should rather recall them to mind continually, and stick to them (which means reaching a better understanding of them, and this requires critical appraisal, and if need be, new orientation). Having made the decision to declare ourselves in a "final way" to a person or way of life, we are actually expressing the firm will to proceed along the way we have begun to the end, and to avoid everything that could possibly deflect us from this.

Because of the consequences of such decisions there is no room for half-heartedness. If two people build a love and life relationship together, it can only succeed to the extent that they are really prepared to trust each other, to be involved with one another, and if need be, to take radical renunciations into account. If the partners have doubts or reservations from the beginning, or lower their sights, there is great danger that they will never find a way to each other. Resolutions that fundamentally alter life demand our total commitment.

"Two Souls dwell within my Breast"

When we speak about decisions, every reservation is disastrous. This is particularly clear in the area of love between people. Love has something unconditional about it. Those who really love can never say to the other: "I am quite fond of you." Or: "I'll love you to the end of the year" Or even: "I'll only love you if you do this for me and give me that." If we love a person we mean: "I love you now and for ever." Love always aims for the eternal.

If we decide to follow Christ, we find ourselves in a similar situation. Here too, we are always concerned with total commitment — we cannot simply decide to give it a try. "No one who puts his hand to the plough and looks back is fit for the kingdom of God" (Lk. 9,62).

In his final rule for his order — confirmed by Pope Honorius III on November 29 1223 — Francis of Assisi refers to these words of Jesus, and reminds his companions that they are "in no way free to withdraw from this bond (of evangelical life within the community of brothers)."[1] Apart from the evangelical counsel to which the order binds itself, does this not also apply to all those who wish to become followers of Jesus? We have to admit that sometimes we view the begging brother from Assisi as a romantic visionary and incurable dreamer, who preached to the birds, and they obviously listened with more patience than the happy-go-lucky Christians of the time. However one may judge him in individual things — a failed social revolutionary, a crafty critic of the church, a mystic far from this world, or all these together — we cannot doubt his literal interpretation of the commitment that Jesus demands of his followers. We are able to hold firm to a decision made for the whole of our future life only if we do not underestimate all possible risks. The Poverello's first rule clearly expresses this sober view; it was confirmed by Pope Innocent III:

"Therefore we brothers, as the Lord said, want to let the dead bury their dead, and be very wary of the wickedness and intrigues of Satan, because he wills that man does not direct his senses and heart to God. He goes around and seeks to take man's heart away under the pretence of reward or assistance, and to wipe out the word and commandment of God from all memory: and he wants to make man's heart blind through worldly doings and sorrows, and dwell within it, as the Lord has said...."[2]

And now Francis quotes a parable, in which Jesus reminds us that the decision to become his followers only represents the first step, but the following itself consists in a life-long way in community with him, and requires ever new *decisions*.

"When the unclean spirit has gone out of a man, he passes through waterless places, seeking rest, but he finds none. Then he says 'I will return to my house from

which I came.' And when he comes he finds it empty, swept and put in order. Then he goes and brings with him seven other spirits more evil than himself, and they enter and dwell there; and the last state of that man becomes worse than the first" (Matt. 12, 43-45; compare Lk. 11,24-26).

In the "Fioretti" (the "Little Flowers of Saint Francis," a collection of pious legends and episodes from his life) one of the saint's visions obviously based on this parable has been handed down. Francis spoke about this parable in his first rule and this may have inspired the unknown author of the "Fioretti" to tell this story.

"Once St. Francis prayed in the monastery of Portiuncula; there he saw through divine revelation how the monastery was completely surrounded by demons, and besieged by a great army. But none of these were able to force their way into the monastery, for the monks were so God-fearing that entrance to them was denied to the demons.

So it remained for a time. But one day one of the brothers became so incensed with another that he thought in his heart how he could accuse him and be able to take his revenge upon him. Because he gave himself up to this wicked thought the devil had free entrance, forced his way into the monastery, and sat himself upon the brother's neck. But when the pious and vigilant shepherd (Francis), who always watched over his sheep, became aware that the wolf had come in order to devour his sheep, he called the monk to him immediately, and commanded him to make known to him at once the reason for this poisonous hatred that he had against his neighbor, because his wrath had handed him over into the hands of his enemy. Then the sinful brother was shocked when he saw how the holy father saw through him, and opened up to him the poisonous anger that filled him, confessed his sin and begged him humbly for penance and mercy. And as he confessed he was freed from his sin and St. Francis ordered the devil to leave. The brother, freed from the clutches of the monster through the goodness of his mild shepherd, thanked God. Instructed and converted, he joined again the flock of the saint, and lived within it in great piety. "[3]

As long as the brothers really live as followers of Jesus, he is the true Lord of the monastery; and for this reason entrance is denied to the demon. But it needs only one of them to allow himself *evil thoughts*, and he drives Jesus out of his heart. The house is empty, the demons get access and sit upon *the brother's neck,* so that he is literally ridden by the devil and totally handed over to him.

It is not the outward actions of a person that are decisive, but what takes place in his heart. "For out of the heart come evil thoughts, murder, adultery, fornication, theft, false witness, slander."(Mt. 15,19)

Doubtless the story of St. Francis's vision aims firstly at pious edification. At the same time though, it is a plausible exegesis of the parable of the unclean spirit.

Jesus's talk of the "unclean spirits" reflects ancient eastern imagery, with its widespread belief in demons; belief in the existence of "unclean spirits" corresponded to a widely held conviction at the time. Equally common was the idea of demons finding no rest in their desert dwellings, and therefore repeatedly trying to possess a person, and establish a residence for evil.

Today many people have a tendency to dismiss such notions with a condescending smile. Even if one sees such imagery as conditioned by the religious and cultural conceptions of that time, it can be demonstrated that it rests upon a solid anthropological foundation.

When is a person "possessed"? When he is not at one with himself. When he allows himself to be determined by forces that hinder his development. When he hunts after phantoms and illusions which make him a stranger to himself. When he thinks he can *make* his happiness by striving after power, success and ownership — and when he is at the same time darkly aware that he could lead another, freer life. Goethe formulates this in Faust:

Two souls dwell, alas, within my breast,
One will from the other part:
One, in coarse lust for love
Clings to the world with clamoring limbs;
The other rises violently from dust
To high ancestral spheres.[4]

It is clear that during his life span man is torn between a yearning for the highest and a tendency towards the lowest. But even when he declares himself for his noblest feelings and makes an effort to lead an almost angelic existence, he is always subject to the temptation to give into his base desires and to lose sight of his ideals.

This is exactly what Jesus reminds us of in his parable. To do this he uses the popular notion of people being the dwelling places of good or bad spirits. Today Faust's words of the "two souls" may appear more appropriate; but both parable and Faust are concerned with the same thing.

Jesus wants us to understand that when we decide to repent and follow him, we must not allow ourselves to be content with our initial enthusiasm. Otherwise,

190

although the house is "swept and put in order," it is "empty." This well-cleaned and empty house forms the dramatic high point of the parable. Although the demon is scared away we are still aware of our destructive tendencies and inwardly distance ourselves from them. *But the house must not remain unlived in, because the unclean spirits will otherwise try to make it their home again.* Now is the time to keep a dwelling place free for the new head of the household. It would be an illusion to want to overcome our bad tendencies without *at the same time* deciding upon a positive framework for life. And according to the New Testament, this happens when one becomes a follower of Christ. That this does not countenance any kind of reservation is explained in a double parable, in which Jesus invites us to evaluate our possibilities realistically and at the same time not to overlook our limitations.

"For which of you, desiring to build a tower, does not first sit down and count the cost, whether he has enough to complete it? Otherwise, when he has laid a foundation, and is not able to finish, all who see it begin to mock him, saying 'this man began to build, and was not able to finish.' Or what king, going to encounter another king in war, will not sit down first and take counsel whether he is able with ten thousand to meet him who comes against him with twenty thousand? And if not, while the other is yet a great way off, he sends an embassy and asks terms of peace" (Lk. 14,28-32).

Naturally every vineyard owner dreams of a "tower" (which we must imagine as a house with stone foundations). And kings dream of victory. And both dreams can only be realized if an effort is made to find the necessary means. In both cases the expenditure is enormous. The vineyard owner must work harder and reduce his expenses, otherwise he can never get the

191

necessary money together. The king is forced to muster soldiers, to double his forces, otherwise he will never defeat his enemy. But should we not also take everything into account if we want to achieve our goal? In his double parable Jesus tells us that we should not overlook difficulties or repress them, but must confront them with the firm purpose of overcoming them.

The goal that Jesus speaks about is the kingdom of God. And this will only be granted to those who follow him without *reservation*. There is no doubt from Jesus's introduction to the double parable of building a tower and waging war that it refers to following him:

"Now great multitudes accompanied him; and he turned and said to them, 'If any one comes to me and does not hate his own father and mother and wife and children and brothers and sisters, yes, and even his own life, he cannot be my disciple" (Lk. 14,25-26).

Here Jesus reminds us that it is not enough to seek his company simply because we feel good in his presence; those of us who think like this are far from being his followers. He demands infinitely more, as the hard word "hate" implies, not only for our closest relations, but for our own lives. The original Greek text speaks of "hatred" *(misein),* an expression that points back to a Hebrew way of speaking. In Hebrew the word "hate" in this context has no emotional ring, but means "to put someone else last" or to "think less of them." What is implied is that even the closest bonds between human beings must not present any hindrance when we are talking about following Jesus.

Such extreme situations, in which someone must make a choice between family ties and following Jesus are to a certain extent the "emergencies" of belief. One does not have to go back to antiquity, when the decision for Christ frequently meant a break with a pagan family, and for a time could even lead to bloody martyrdom. Many Christians found themselves faced with a similar dilemma at the time of the Third Reich. Should they have taken an active part in building up an unjust state, compromise, or simply keep silent? Or were they not committed to declare their positions, in view of the monstrous crimes against humanity according to international law? When making such a decision, everyone was aware that one not only endangered one's own life, but also the lives of all relatives as at that time there was the infamous law of families being liable for the crimes of one member.

Even these few examples make it abundantly clear what Jesus means by following him: because we are concerned with what is essential, our total commitment is demanded. If we shrink back from it we should have no illusions; every hesitation leads to pitiful failure. For this reason it does us good to remind ourselves constantly of the half-finished tower in the vineyard and of the victory that the king missed. These parables are meant only to make us aware that we must change our lives fundamentally if we are to be fully human.

An everyday example may make this clearer. A young woman asks her fiancé what he actually expects and wants from her. He replies that he expects her to be ever loving towards him, cook his meals, do his washing, keep the house in order, in short he expects her to be a good housewife and remain faithful to him. If the woman still wants to marry him she really doesn't deserve anything better. What do you want of me? There is only one answer to this question: what do I want of you? Not just *something* but quite simply *you, and that is completely.* What else could I wish for except that you return the devotion that I feel for you, that you love me with every fibre of your being, as I love you?

What does Jesus want of his people when he invites them to follow him? Not merely a couple of prayers or a couple of good works, or a couple of listless religious gymnastic exercises. First and above all he wants our hearts, in other words: our *belief.* It is not by chance that the Latin word for belief *credere* goes back to the concept *cor dare*, which means *to give one's heart.* So Jesus's request to follow him is nothing other than an invitation to believe.

It lies in the nature of the thing that this belief demanded by Jesus allows no room for limitations or reservations. There is no doubt about this in the Hebrew Bible, to which Jesus constantly refers in his proclamation. Again and again the subject there is the safe support that man finds in God alone. This fact is described with the verb *aman* which means "be firm," "be based," "support yourself upon something." *Aman*, (from which our liturgical word "Amen" comes) confirms that something holds to what it has promised. Applied to Jahweh-God it signifies that he keeps his promises, and will stay true to man through all possible dangers. The one who believes can therefore trust himself entirely to God because he can always depend upon him.

Such a belief leaves no room for any kind of objection or doubt. And it was so with Abraham who, at a great age and trusting in God's promise, left his homeland to move into an unknown country. The same is true of the chosen people, who on God's word departed from the land of Egypt and went towards an uncertain future, thereby placing all their hopes upon God's support alone. In the same way the belief required by Jesus always is and remains a hazardous undertaking that demands unconditional commitment from a person. Following Jesus does not represent an occupation alongside others, but is meant to transform our entire human existence.

Jesus does not put an unbearable burden on his followers: "For my yoke is easy, and my burden is light" (Mt. 12,30). Using these words he takes up the familiar images of the time: the "yoke of the law," the "yoke of the Torah," or the "yoke of the Holy," which were used by the contemporary rabbis.[5] This yoke not only protected the Israelites from the snare of their own passions, but also from the subjugation by other peoples. When Jesus calls upon us to follow him, he pursues a similar intention; he wants to protect us from poisoning our souls and losing our hearts, so that in the end we do not sit upon the ruins of our unfinished towers or have to mourn a failed victory.

Excessive Demands?

Are Jesus's demands *excessive*? Do we not discover again and again that in spite of all serious resolutions we lag behind our good intentions, and that we never stick consistently to our promises? "For a righteous man falls seven times, and rises again" (Prov. 24,16). Perhaps this insight from the biblical proverb reflects our own experiences?

Both the double parable of the building of the tower and of waging war and that of the unclean spirit seem to exclude the thought of a possible relapse. In this respect the legend of St. Francis is more realistic. We are expressly told that the fallible brother sinned *after* he had decided to follow Jesus in the order, and that once again he made his way *back* along the right path.

Of course Jesus also takes account of the fact that the firm will to follow him does not exclude relapses.

It is precisely for this reason that he not only warns his disciples but also the crowds that gather around him to beg God continually for forgiveness (Mt. 5,1; 6,12).

The fact that there can be setbacks is not debated in the three parables. They are only concerned with the seriousness of the decision and must not be weakened by the thought of possible failure. Those of us who *calculate* on setbacks *right from the beginning* have decided on compromise, and have already given in to any possible difficulties.

A comparison: can everything work out well if a man and a woman come together to form a lasting partnership, but at the same time are not prepared to renounce the freedom and independence that in all probability represent a danger to their mutual fidelity? Will they be able — or want — to sustain their relationship if right from the start they have played with the idea of separating when serious arguments, crises or difficulties become apparent? Will they be at all able to build up a true relationship if they have not basically tested whether they "have enough to complete it?" At first the parables of the tower and of waging war may seem harsh; but are they unrealistic?

The author of the legend of St. Francis writes from a totally different perspective. He does not speculate as to whether we could — or should — set the standard for our behavior a little lower, but sensibly sees that, in spite of all good will, man is constantly weak. In view of this fact he considers how we can bring the one at fault back to the right path without exposing him or unnecessarily humiliating him. To achieve this he uses the image of the good shepherd for Francis: "Instructed and converted he joined again the flock of the saint, and lived within it in great piety."

Of course in everyday life this process of repentance takes a little longer. A woman who trusts her husband unreservedly and whose trust is violated by her abandonment feels debased and worthless. Must this woman see herself as a bad Christian because she simply cannot (or cannot *yet*) forgive her husband? It is important that she first work through her disappointment inwardly. She will hardly be able to break down her quite understandable feelings of bitter resentment moment after moment. That demands time. It seems that the author of the St. Francis legend does not consider the psychological patterns of behavior that are at work in such a case. He neither mentions the reason why the monk suddenly starts hating a fellow-brother, nor does he attempt to explain how it would be possible to overcome this hatred from the start. This is understandable, because his intention is aimed at re-calling the Christian *ideal* of brotherly love and readiness to forgive to the minds of his readers.

Meanwhile the realization of this ideal always represents a *goal*. One must never lose sight of this. What is important is the continuous struggle. It is only this that allows us to measure whether, and to what extent, a person actually makes the effort to tread in Jesus's footsteps. Even the most zealous Christian can never succeed in following Jesus's instruction that says "You therefore, must be perfect as your heavenly Father is perfect" (Mt. 5,58). Here too we are concerned with a commandment that sets a goal. One can get nearer to this goal. But one can also distance oneself from it.

Jesus's instructions may be likened to the milestones along the way that leads to God. The Nobel prizewinner Isaac Bashevis Singer illustrates in his novel "The Penitent" that there are numerous stumbling blocks along this way. Singer's theme, of course, is not that of following Jesus, but a return to the Jewish faith of the fathers.

Joseph Shapiro is a Jew who fled from Europe to the USA. He is a highly respected New York businessman who enjoys all the luxuries of modern life. He becomes increasingly aware of the fact that he moves in a cynical and apathetic society. After many self doubts he flees from his unfaithful wife (he has also deceived her), and from his mistress Liza (who has used him) and from her voracious daughter to Israel, with the firm intention of leading a life of faith there, according to the tradition of his forbears.

But during the flight to Tel Aviv he meets an easygoing woman; all his good intentions threaten to come to nothing: later he remembers this episode with great shame.

"It seems that the Evil Spirit or Satan was anxious to show someone in Heaven that all my vows and resolutions had been worthless." [6]

Shapiro meets a great many old acquaintances in Tel Aviv, and they introduce him to a society that actually does not differ greatly from his New York life, and this makes it difficult for him to give up his old habits:

"I had fled from Celia and Liza but I was again surrounded by countless Celias and Lizas, real ones and potential ones. I knew from all these invitations and meetings with female friends would come the sort of life that I was trying to escape. I already had offers of an affair from a few married women. The faith that had been ignited within me during the worst crisis of my life began to cool and become extinguished. I stood in the synagogue ostensibly praying, but the words had ceased to comfort and convince me."

The actual changing of his ways happens later, when Shapiro meets Reb Chaim in a study house. During the evening meal which follows in this rabbi's house (where he meets the latter's daughter Sarah for the first time), Shapiro has a key experience:

"Fate had tossed me from Celia, Liza, and Priscilla back to true Jewishness, to the source from which we had all drunk, back onto the path that led to the Torah and to purity. "

His explanation reads like a modern paraphrase of the parable of the unclean spirit.

"This was the first day that I lived like a Jew. The Evil Spirit had been silenced, but I knew that he would presently regain his tongue. Sure enough, I soon heard him say 'All this would be fine if you were a true believer, but actually, you are nothing more than a heretic afflicted with nostalgia. You will soon turn back to your heretic ways, and what's more, you'll bring nothing but grief to a pious Jewish daughter. You won't be able to stand her for long. You'll get tired of her in one month, or, at the most, three.'

'I'll marry her and I'll stay with her,' I said in reply to the Glib One. 'I'll be a Jew whether you approve of it or not. He who despises evil must believe in holiness.'

'I've seen a lot of such penitents as you' Satan countered. 'It's no more than a passing fancy. They always go back to what they were.'

'If I can't be a Jew, I'll put an end to my life!' I shouted within me.

'These are the words of a modern man' an imp whispered in my ear.

I went to bed, but I lay for hours unable to sleep. I had fallen in love with Sarah, my present wife and the mother of my children. "

199

The realization with which Singer finishes his novel is in accord with both Jesus and Judaism. Changing one's ways represents a decision which does not merely affect some areas of human existence, but the whole of life — and during the course of an entire life one must repeat this decision ever anew.

"The Evil Spirit hasn't been liquidated. Even as I sit there and study the Gemara, I think idle thoughts more befitting a wastrel. A moment doesn't pass without temptations. Satan is constantly on the attack. He never gets tired."

He never gets tired; one must constantly be armored, and relapses are possible at any time: this view is the basis of a proverb that Jesus certainly knew — we have already quoted half of it. *"For a righteous man falls seven times, and rises again; but the wicked are overthrown by calamity"* (Prov. 24,16). To put it another way: only the godless person, who goes his own way, counts as wicked. But he who makes an effort to obey God's instructions, counts as "righteous," however often he fails. It therefore becomes clear that not only the decision to follow, that is, the "conversion," but following itself must be understood as a process, which only reaches its end at a person's death.

Not one of us can assume that we possess belief for ever. It is far more the case that every believer knows only too well that he must constantly pray that belief will take possession of him again and again.

This is the reason why the saints particularly often describe themselves as the greatest sinners. We refer once more to Francis. When one of his fellow brothers once asked him what he thought of himself, he answered: "I believe I am the greatest sinner that runs about the world."[7]

This coincides with what the chronicler says elsewhere:

"When Saint Francis was praised and it was said of him that he was a saint, he usually answered such talk in the following way: 'Until today I am not certain that I will not have sons and daughters; then as soon as the Lord wishes to withdraw the treasure he has entrusted to me, what would remain left to me except a body and a soul, and non-believers have these too? Yes, I have to say to myself that if the Lord had shown a robber or a non-believer such goodness as he has shown to me, they would be more faithful to him than I am."

Such statements show that following Jesus can never be fully realized, and the goal never completely reached. At the same time we are reminded that there are no perfect or imperfect people before God, but only the needy, who all rely upon his grace. The difference is simply whether one is aware of this or not.

10

At the Foot of the Cross

Compared to other great movements in world history, Christianity seems a most unlikely one indeed, all the more so when we consider the teaching and life of its founder — one who was born in a stable and died on the gallows, one who taught that "whoever would save his life will lose it and whoever loses his life for my sake will find it" (Mt. 16,25; Jn. 12,25).

Certainly his preaching of God's all-embracing love and above all his selfless commitment to the poor and those deprived of rights enabled him to convince a few Galilean rustics. But at least for a time the distrustful and organized opposition of the established religious administration was more successful in suppressing than his followers were in spreading the proclamation of his message. Although Jesus must soon have been clear about the failure of his mission — that is, the conversion of Israel — he still went unwaveringly upon his way until death. Only after his disciples had to some extent overcome their consternation about this were they gradually able to convince themselves that his life indeed showed the right way to become fully human — and that those who go this way have to expect every kind of opposition.

Watering down the Message?

Simple folk piety developed a sixth sense for what was correct and true. Jesus's birthplace was not adorned with any symbols of ruling power; the child in the manger was simply provided in folklore with an ox and an ass. But there is nothing about this in New Testament accounts of his childhood. It is more likely that the custom goes back to the 4th century non-testamental legends of Jesus's birth by the author known to scholars only as the pseudo-Matthew:

"Three days after the birth of our Lord Jesus Christ, Mary left the grotto (in which she had given birth), and made her way to a stable. There she laid the child in a manger, and the ox and the ass worshipped him. Thus was the word of the prophet Isaiah fulfilled; 'The ox knows its owner, and the ass its master's crib...'" (Is. 1,3). [1]

One of these two animals in the manger appears again when Jesus rides into Jerusalem upon the colt of an ass two days before his death (Mt. 21,1-9). Here too the Hebrew Bible is the source. Matthew expressly refers to the prophets Isaiah and Zechariah:

"Tell the daughter of Zion, Behold your king is coming to you, humble, and mounted on an ass, and on a colt, the foal of an ass" (Mt. 21,5; compare Is. 62,11; Zech. 9,9). Jesus does not ride into the center of Jerusalem upon a horse (horses were used in war at the time) but upon an ass, thereby proclaiming that his "rule" excludes any claim to secular power.

Very soon people were making fun of such a savior of the world, who then went on to end up on the cross. Among other things we see this in a derisory crucifix that was found in 1856 in a house in the near neighborhood of the Roman emperors' palace on the Palatine

Hill. The small graffiti, scarcely fifteen centimeters high, may be from the first half of the third century. It shows the crucified one with an ass's head, before him a man looking up to him. Underneath is written in Greek: "Alexamenos worships his God." Another graffiti of a little man with the inscription "Alexamenos fidelis — the Christian believer Alexamenos," found in 1870 in the same room documents that this Alexamenos, otherwise unknown to us, professed Christianity. Today this graffiti which mocks at Christianity as stupidity (the ass's head) can be seen in the *Antiquarium* on the Palatine Hill. It is presumably the oldest representation of the crucifixion.

It took time before the Christians themselves dared to show images of the suffering and humiliated Jesus. This fear of depicting the crucifixion, which was considered shameful, persisted until the sixth century; only a few images representing it have been preserved from this time. Later scenes of the crucifixion show a standing or throned victorious king upon the tree of life. It was only at the beginning of the 13th century, when Franciscan spirituality gained greater influence, that representations of the tortured Christ hanging upon the martyr's tree began to increase, and at first they were considered heretical and incompatible with the dignity of the redeemer.

This is only too easily understood. That a failure, hanging powerless upon the cross should, of all people, be the savior of humanity, borders, if you look at it calmly, upon madness.

This was how Paul himself found this teaching of faith when he had already come to terms with it. According to purely human measures of success it seemed foolish to him to suggest Jesus's way for himself and others. The shock that this knowledge gave him is shown in the often quoted lines that he wrote to the community in Corinth: "...but we preach Christ crucified, a stumbling block to the Jews, and folly to Gentiles.." (I Cor. 1,23).

A stumbling block to the Jews: according to Jewish interpretation a hanged man was cursed by God. When crucifixion was introduced in Palestine as the death punishment under Roman rule, this opinion, found in a passage of Deuteronomy (see 21,22-23), was also applied to the person condemned upon the cross. This was reason enough for belief in Jesus as the Messiah to pose a stumbling block to every Jew at the time.

A folly to gentiles: The Roman statesman and philosopher Cicero (106-43 BC) also states that death on the cross was considered the greatest humiliation that could be afflicted upon a person: "Not only the bodies of Roman citizens, but also their thoughts, their eyes, and their ears must remain protected from this."[2] Understandably it was forbidden to employ this form of death punishment on the citizens of the Empire.

In view of this, Paul feels obliged to explain: "but to those who are called, both Jews and Greeks, Christ the power of God and the wisdom of God. For the foolishness of God is wiser than men, and the weakness of God is stronger than men" (1.Cor. 1, 24-5).

These sentences are reassuringly edifying but the briefest glance at church history reveals a discrepancy between belief and practice. Admiration for Christ has frequently overshadowed the imitation of Christ. Claims to power have taken precedence over the behavior such imitation requires, establishing a "holy rule" more important than putting the evangelical counsels into practice. Were people then — as well as now — inclined to wear the cross around their necks as a decoration rather then carrying it as a burden upon their backs?

The Danish philosopher Søren Kierkegaard frequently pointed to this painful contrast between academic truth and the truth that is really lived. Here is a short passage from the journal "The Moment" which he published at his own expense; it is not by chance that Kierkegaard quotes Paul:

"The noble and glorious High Preacher to the High Court appears in the magnificent cathedral, the chosen favorite of the chosen few. He appears before the chosen circle of the chosen and preaches movingly on a text he has chosen himself: 'God chose the least in the world, and the despised!' And no one there laughed." [3]

Kierkegaard is understandingly puzzled that Christianity can proclaim the kingdom of God *and* at the same time come to terms with the rich of this world.

Imitating or Following?

Jesus's conception of following takes a totally different direction:

"You are the salt of the earth; but if salt has lost its taste, how shall its saltness be restored? It is no longer good for anything except to be thrown out and trodden under foot by men.

You are the light of the world. A city set on a hill cannot be hid. Nor do men light a lamp and put it under a bushel, but on a stand, and it gives light to all in the house. Let your light so shine before men, that they may see your good works and give glory to your father who is in heaven." (Mt 5,13-16; compare Mk. 9,50 and 4,21; Lk. 14,34-35 and 8,16).

The two passages about salt (Mk. 9,50; Lk. 14,34) and about light (Mk. 4,21; Lk. 8,16) were originally handed down separately, but here Matthew combines them with imagery that links them together and puts them into the Sermon on the Mount (see Mt. 5,1-12). The statement is clear; the gospel is a gift — but at the same time a task. Jesus then elucidates the two images of the light of the world and the salt of the earth by means of a parable:

"For it will be (with the kingdom of God) as when a man going on a journey called his servants and entrusted to them his property; to one he gave five talents, to another two, to another one, to each according to his ability. Then he went away. He who had received the five talents went at once and traded with them; and he made five talents more. So also, he who had the two talents made two talents more. But he who had received the one talent went and dug in the ground and hid his master's money. Now after a long time the master of those servants came and settled accounts with them. And he who had received the five talents came forward, bringing five talents more, saying 'Master, you delivered to me five talents; here I have made five talents more.' His master said to him 'Well done, good and faithful servant; you have been faithful over a little, I will set you over much; enter into the joy of your master.' And he also who had the two talents came forward, saying, 'Master, you delivered to me two talents; here I have made two talents more.' His master said to him, 'Well done, good and faithful servant; you have been faithful over a little; I will set you over much; enter into the joy of your master.' He also who had received the one talent came forward, saying 'Master, I knew you to be a hard man, reaping where you did not sow, and gathering where you did not winnow; so

I was afraid, and I went out and hid your talent in the ground. Here you have what is yours.' But his master answered him 'You wicked and slothful servant! You knew that I reap where I have not sowed, and gather where I have not winnowed? Then you ought to have invested my money with the bankers, and at my coming I should have received what was my own with interest. So take the talent from him and give it to him who has the ten talents. For to everyone who has will more be given, and he will have abundance; but from him who has not, even what he has will be taken away. And cast the worthless servant into the outer darkness; there men will weep and gnash their teeth.'" (Mt. 25,14-30; compare Lk. 19, 12-27).*

In its present form this parable goes back to the evangelist, who applies it to Christ's second coming and the happiness at the end of time ("Enter into the joy of your master!") for which the disciples could hope. After Jesus's departure (after his "ascension") the Christian community not only has to manage his inheritance until the end of time, but also increase it. Setting aside the imagery, the responsibility which is linked to receiving the good tidings is emphatically called to mind. At the same time the evangelist reminds his readers of the coming judgment, and warns them not to forfeit eternal salvation. However, this interpretation shifts the original main focus of the story.

We can see how this has been re-worked by the evangelist. Matthew replaces the mina (pound) of Luke's version with the talent. A mina was worth one hundred denarii, and a denarius roughly corresponded to the daily wage of a simple worker at that time. But in Matthew the first worker is given five talents, which correspond to thirty thousand denarii or eighty years wages. The assumption is based on the fact that both versions go back to a common model.[4] If we compare both the versions, we find a mutual basis, which probably molded the original form of the parable told by Jesus himself: a man takes himself off on a long journey and trusts some of his servants with a sum of money corresponding to their abilities. Naturally he expects that they will put the money to work. One of them simply puts it aside (according to Matthew he buries it because it is a considerable sum, according to Luke he keeps it in a napkin). He does so because he fears his master. The latter picks up the argument: if you already think that I reap where I have not sowed, should you not then for this reason alone have taken the money to the bank, where it would at least have acquired interest?

Jesus's fellow countrymen would have understood at once what he wanted to say in this story; do not keep God's good tidings to yourself. Rather proclaim it to all other people, so that they may also be inspired by it.

Following the Cross?

The considerable difficulties involved in this task were first experienced to the full by the disciples after Jesus's death and resurrection. They were totally prepared to adopt his way of life as their own. It must have been clear to them quite soon that following him also implied readiness to share his destiny, if necessary, even his passion.

It is, however, difficult to attribute the references to carrying the cross, as they are handed down to us, to Jesus himself, for they presume his death upon the cross: "Whoever does not bear his own cross and come after me, cannot be my disciple" (Lk. 14,27). These words reflect the experiences of the disciples that we are later told about extensively in the Acts of the

Apostles: ostracism, pursuit, imprisonment, torture, and every conceivable kind of persecution.

However, by putting these words into Jesus's mouth in his gospel "....If any man would come after me, let him deny himself and take up his cross *daily* and follow me" (Lk. 9,23), the author of the Acts of the Apostles states precisely that following the cross is not just a practice for exceptional circumstances. In contrast to Matthew (16,24) and Mark (8,34), Luke speaks of a *daily* cross, thus giving us the key to interpreting these often misleading and indeed misunderstood words.

Is it not the case that we often hear in church proclamation that as Christians we are bound to *seek* the cross? However, this kind of renunciation for renunciation's sake lacks any biblical foundation; at most it is of interest to psychotherapists.

First of all, the words about following the cross daily demand that we should not repress experience of suffering from consciousness, but should work through it. This refers to the suffering that lies like a dark shadow over almost every human life: a bad past, that one humps around like a burden; a terrible guilt that cannot be dispelled; the often shattering consciousness of failure and misery, and the knowledge that we are never quite wholly ourselves because we are never quite whole. Everyone has this kind of experience. We want to be someone else, we don't feel well anymore in our own skins, we can't stand the sight of ourselves. Such realizations are painful and all too often lead to rejection of self and to hatred of self (and this is then expressed in feelings of hatred and rejection towards others).

In this connection following the cross means working through what oppresses us and is difficult, confronting ourselves in our deepest thoughts, in dialogue with friends, and in the face of God. Learning to accept our insufficiencies and our limitations is perhaps one of the most difficult tasks put upon us. It is not just a day to day task but a wearisome progress, often very painful; put in religious terms, we are talking about a cross that is laid upon us.

More than this, following the cross includes the readiness to bear suffering. Here we mean the suffering that is unavoidable, in the face of which we become radically aware of our powerlessness. Someone may have an incurable disease and knows all too well that even the best doctors cannot help. Or a relationship of many years standing breaks up suddenly because the wife tells her husband that she now loves another, and there is no question of her coming back. A man's whole existence can be threatened because the firm he has worked for for decades rationalizes away a couple of hundred jobs to save money. Or someone who has always accepted you and been able to give you a feeling of home suddenly dies....we could go on and on counting the experiences of pain that often darken our lives for years. The Christian tries to carry this pain as he prays, like Jesus (and with him), "Father, thy will be done."

For those who are serious about carrying the cross all suffering represents a challenge of such nature that for them there is no more foreign pain. Anyone calling upon Jesus cannot possibly go his own way, but follows Jesus upon *his* way, and thus to the pain of the needy, the poor and the weak, the despised and those cheated of life. This is the reason why in the view of the authorities Jesus had to die upon the cross. Through his solidarity with sinners (and also with those who were *considered* sinners because they did not know the law's instructions and therefore could not follow them), he endangered the ruling religious system and thereby the

211

position of the religious leaders, who endeavored to push him aside.[5]

If we talk frequently today of the changing nature of religious activity this does not necessarily mean that religion is to be seen as something to correct abuses in society. Christian authorities especially have often endeavored to maintain the status quo of society. Instead of denouncing obvious abuses they sometimes serve to legitimize them, often employing labyrinthine arguments. For example, foreign affairs are not discussed at the levels of justice and basic human rights but the emphasis is often put on the commandment to love and therefore divine order itself requires that we turn first of all to those nearest us, to our own families, our relations and our own countrymen. But a *following of Jesus* that merely serves to protect our own rights shows a perversion of that *following of the cross* to which Jesus calls his people. A society that is to a large degree not orientated towards *being* but towards *having* will rejoice when the churches prescribe their members sedatives instead of administering the salt of the earth to them. Johann Baptist Metz has constantly drawn our attention to this danger.

"Where Christianity gives in to this pressure from society, although it may become more acceptable in high places, I fear it will develop even more into a 'bourgeois religion,' to which our society...also gives the green light to live as it itself lives. An authentic return to religion, on the other hand, must be a return to changing one's ways, a return to the messianic practice of love. It may be that that which love here demands seems like betrayal: betrayal of wealth, family, and the normal order of life. But it may also be that this is precisely the area of differentiation between the minds at work in the churches of the rich and powerful

212

countries in the world. It is true, Christianity is not
merely there for the brave. However, it is not we who
define the unreasonable demands of love; and it is not
we who put forward the conditions under which love is
tested. So it is that in times of nationalistic thought
Christian love must carry the suspicion of national
dishonor. In times of racism it will draw the suspicion
of race betrayal down upon itself. And in times of social
contrasts in the world that cry to heaven, it will draw
down upon itself the suspicion of class betrayal in the
supposedly plausible interests of those who own." [6]

In fact, those who respect God's power will have no
truck with the powerful of this world, but will make
themselves strong for the weak; and those who allow
themselves to be led by God's spirit will find it impossible to conform to the "Zeitgeist." The conflict with
those who are only concerned with their own advan-
tages and never with the well-being of their fellow
human beings is then virtually pre-programmed.

Anyone who lives his faith consistently can never
bear to settle at ease between lazy compromises. If you
start off on the way with Jesus, you can not only expect
some uncomfortable moments, but also the frequent
loss of social recognition and public reputation. In
short, following Jesus simply implies following the
cross. Understood in this way, following is not synonymous with mere imitation of his actions, but also takes
circumstances into account. Jesus himself illustrates in
a picaresque story that those who wish to follow in his
footsteps must have more than their fair share of fantasy
and original ideas. This story probably made his listeners smile at first, and then reflect.

"There was a rich man who had a steward, and charges
were brought up to him that this man was wasting his
goods. And he called him and said to him, 'What is this

that I hear about you? Turn in the account of your stewardship, for you can no longer be steward.' And the steward said to himself, 'What shall I do, since my master is taking the stewardship away from me? I am not strong enough to dig, and I am ashamed to beg. I have decided what to do, so that people may receive me into their houses when I am put out of the stewardship.' So, summoning his master's debtors one by one, he said to the first 'How much do you owe my master?' He said 'A hundred measures of oil.' And he said to him 'Take your bill, and sit down quickly and write fifty.' Then he said to another, 'And how much do you owe?' He said 'A hundred measures of wheat.' He said to him, 'Take your bill, and write eighty.' The master commended the dishonest steward for his shrewdness; for the sons of this world are more shrewd in dealing with their own generation than the sons of light" (Lk. 16,1-8).

This does not simply tell us the story of a roguish prank, but depicts a case of business criminality. The steward not only severely damages the property owner through criminal mismanagement, he also incites the debtors to falsify their bills in order to get them involved. And the sums that they will save on these invoices are certainly not small! Fifty measures of oil correspond to 475 gallons; eighty sacks of wheat to more than 1200 pounds. When it is simply a matter of surviving, every means can be employed.

Of course the person who holds this swindler and charlatan up as an example should not be identified with the rich man, who is actually cheated twice. It is the narrator of this story who invites his disciples (see Lk. 16,1; "He also said to the disciples") to take a leaf out of this cheat's book.

However, the point of comparison is not the unscrupulous behavior of this swindler with no conscience, but his shrewdness and cunning. Jesus is of the opinion that the "sons of light" can learn something here from the "sons of this world." The following to which he calls us must always be practiced under the respective social assumptions and conditions of society; it has a creative and innovative character. We are not simply asked for passive virtues like humility, sacrifice, and the readiness to renounce, but *equally* for the spirit of sacrifice linked to rich ideas, innovation and the power of imagination. In short, Jesus does not call us to sterile imitation, but to follow him creatively. People like Mother Teresa, Martin Luther King or Abbé Pierre have been able to put such following into practice.

Working for peace, for solidarity with the people of the Third World, striving for better working conditions for the employed and caring for the homeless, the handicapped and the unemployed, defending the rights of conscientious objectors to military service, the dignity of women and their position in the church, seeking changes in church legislation for a greater voice in the appointment of bishops, for greater freedom in theological research and community celebration of the eucharist — all of these are related to justice, love of one's neighbor and consequently with the following of Christ.

In a few simple words Francis of Assisi tells us at the beginning of his order's rules what following Jesus signifies: "the rules and the lives of the brothers are to preserve the holy gospel of Our Lord Jesus Christ..." This really says everything, but because he is dealing with the order of the friars minor, Francis naturally also commits them to the evangelical counsel: "...through a life of obedience without possessions, and of chastity."[7] We know that in his radical following of Jesus the merchant's son from Assisi brought about a revolution within the Christianity of his time. While most of the spiritual dignitaries were using the gospels as props for power, Francis took Jesus's words so literally that people actually saw a "second Christ" in him. It is therefore understandable that legends about him were circulating shortly after his death in 1226 (some of them quite far fetched). They show parallels between the man from Nazareth and the begging brother from Assisi. According to some legends, the saint's mother also gave birth to him in a stable; he went to Rome — the Jerusalem of the day — with twelve apostles (and not, as history says, with eleven); he fasted for thirty-nine days in humility not to outdo Christ's forty days; he raised a dead man to life, and appeared to his fellow monks as formerly Christ had appeared to the apostles. About 1390 Bartolomeo of Pisa finished a work about the "similarities between the lives of St. Francis and Lord Jesus Christ," in which he analyzed forty resemblances between Francis and Jesus of Nazareth in over a thousand pages.

This sort of hagiographic effort can foster the misunderstanding that following Jesus implied a kind of slavish imitation of him, especially among the favorite saints of Christianity. However, this thought was far from the intention of Franciscan writers. In their search for biographical resemblances between Jesus and Francis of Assisi they were solely concerned to prove that it is not beyond our human possibilities to take the following of Christ to heart, and the gospel at its word.

11
"We are Beggars"

For many of us even the thought of being dependent upon someone else or being in their debt is unbearable.[1] This has something to do with the fact that we have almost forgotten how to ask for things within a relationship. We do not want to become a burden to anyone; we have to get through alone. And if we are really forced to ask a friend to do us a favor, we tend to return it as soon as possible, so that everything is in order again. Order in this case means no need of help from anyone else, standing on one's own feet, being independent.

But even if we convince ourselves that we can manage on our own and control our own lives, in reality we are dependent upon our fellow human beings. This is shown by the banal fact that we cannot even thank ourselves for our own existence. And we can only bring joy and light into our lives by turning towards another person. An understanding look, evidence of sympathy, or a friendly smile can work magic; they show us that others are not completely indifferent towards us.

Objections, Doubts, Questions

Everyone needs recognition and love. We can see in children that their behavior is to a great extent controlled by the most fearful of all anxieties, that of being rejected and unloved. And a person whom nobody

217

cares for becomes stunted. But sympathy, understanding and love can never be forced. They are always *gifts* that we have no right to ask for; we can only receive them thankfully from those who reach out a hand and open their hearts to us.

Whenever another person shows us friendship, devotion or love, we find that we no longer have any inhibitions or reservations about *asking* for something. On the contrary, we are happy to have someone whom we can turn to in difficulty and need, without fear of being refused or having to think of returning the favor. This only happens in a relationship of friendship and trust. The more viable a relationship is, the less we hesitate to ask for help. There is no thought of humiliation or embarrassment.

Another question naturally arises from this: why do some believers in need of help find it humiliating to appear before *God*? It probably harks back to the need to fend for themselves in their human relationships, which is then unconsciously projected onto their relationship with God. If we can only think of ourselves in our daily lives as not dependent upon anyone else, it is understandable that we also do not want to appear as beggars before God. Obviously the same psychic mechanisms are triggered in both cases. As long as we find it humiliating to put our pleas before God, our relationship with him is disturbed.

God accepts every human being in spite of his shortcomings and weaknesses, and therefore we do not have to be ashamed to carry our helplessness and needs to him. Our attitude towards what we ask for in our prayer then becomes an important gauge for intensity of belief.

However, this raises an objection of a social and ethical kind, that has to be taken seriously. Would it not be more honest to limit our pleas to God to asking his pardon for all our transgressions instead of preparing an itemized list of our failings. Could not this give rise to the suspicion that this sort of prayer is nothing less than flight from one's own responsibility, a kind of alibi for wasted chances and missed opportunities?

Bertolt Brecht devoted a whole scene of his play "Mother Courage and her Children" to this subject.

During the Thirty Years' War the Kaiser's troops threaten the Protestant town of Halle. Mother Courage has gone into the town for supplies, leaving her daughter Kattrin, who is mute, with some peasants outside the town. In the middle of the night they are awakened by soldiers who threaten to kill all the cattle if the peasants' son will not show them the way to the town. Unnoticed by the soldiers Kattrin seizes a drum, climbs up onto the roof of the stable, pulling the ladder up after her. The two peasants confine themselves to pleading to God to rescue their relations in the town. But Kattrin begins to beat her drum to wake the townspeople from sleep and warn them of the approaching danger.

PEASANT: Stop beating your drum, you crazy cripple!
WIFE: The soldiers will come.
SERGEANT: [comes running in with his soldiers and the young peasant son] *I'll cut you to pieces!*
WIFE: Officer, we are not guilty, we can't do anything about her. She climbed up there by herself. She doesn't belong to us. She's a stranger.
SERGEANT: Where is the ladder?
PEASANT: Up there!
SERGEANT: [calling up] *This is an order! Throw down the drum!* [Kattrin goes on drumming.] *You are all involved. You won't live to tell about it.*
FIRST SOLDIER: .... Listen, I've got a good suggestion. Come down immediately and go into the town with

219

us. *Show us your mother and we'll spare her.* [Kattrin goes on drumming.]

SERGEANT: I can't stand this anymore. I'll shoot her down, even if that's the last thing I do. Bring me the musket!

[Two soldiers run off, Kattrin goes on drumming.]

WIFE: I know what to do Sergeant. Her cart is over there. If we smash it to pieces she will stop. That's all she has.

SERGEANT: [to the young peasant] *Smash it up!* [to Kattrin] *We'll smash up your cart if you don't stop drumming!*

[The young peasant gives the cart a couple of weak blows with a plank.]

WIFE: Stop that drumming you beast!

[Kattrin stares at her cart and whimpers, but she goes on drumming.]

THE YOUNG PEASANT: [suddenly throwing away the plank]:

Go on drumming! Otherwise they will all be lost! Go on, go on.....

[The soldiers come in with the musket.]

SERGEANT: Get ready! Get ready! [To Kattrin, as the rifle is put in position] *For the last time, Stop that drumming!* [Weeping, Kattrin drums as loudly as she can.] *Fire!* [The soldiers shoot, Kattrin is hit, she beats her drum once or twice more, and then slowly collapses.] *Stop that noise!* [The last beats of the drum are drowned by cannon from the town. In the distance alarm bells are heard and the thunder of cannon.]

FIRST SOLDIER: She has done it.[2]

Our attention is drawn by two parallels here. Both Kattrin's mother and the peasants' relations are in the threatened town. Both Kattrin and the peasants will risk their livelihood (the cart, the farmyard and the cattle) and their lives if they warn the townspeople. While the peasants resort to prayer, Kattrin decides to act, and thereby brings about a change of heart in the young peasant. At first he is prepared to show the soldiers the way, but then following Kattrin's example, he decides on active resistance ("Go on drumming! Otherwise they'll all be lost!")

Obviously Brecht wants to teach us something in this scene. In the end the characters who are praying only ask God to get them out of such a jam, because they themselves are too comfortable or too cowardly or incapable — or all these together — of doing anything themselves. Pleas and petitions excuse them from personal commitment. Prayer develops into an excuse for human passivity or into a magic formula, by means of which one tries to move God to act. In short, petitionary prayer amounts only to self-deception and assuaging one's fear and bad conscience.

This caricature of petitionary prayer becomes the yardstick by which we judge it. Prayer can be interpreted as an alternative to action just as faith can be understood as an authorization to flee from worldly affairs instead of a stimulus to work energetically to improve mankind's material welfare. But whenever these misunderstandings occur, the idea of Christian prayer becomes distorted and contradictory to true Christian life. Everyone who prays should realize that he must follow Jesus's example of practicing what he preached, and understand his service to the poor and the sick, to the outcasts and the sinners. This is the very touchstone and criterion of his inner relationship to God the Father.

Petitionary prayers do not absolve us of responsibility for further action on our own behalf. Furthermore, praying for others is an expression of solidarity; at the

221

same time every petition is a program that should be put into action. We can fold our hands together in prayer with a clear conscience only if we are prepared to open ourselves to the suffering of our fellow human beings.

Is Prayer Necessary?

Naturally we then ask ourselves whether practical commitment is not enough. Why pray as well?

In prayers of petition the believer puts his whole existence, his wishes, his yearnings, and — why do we not admit this openly? — his helplessness before God.

Whenever we confess our needs to God we take account of the fact that in this world, in spite of all safeguards, there is no final security, and at the same time we admit to our belief that this God cares for everyone and everything; that it is he who directs and leads the way of the world and human destiny. In extreme desolation we can rely upon him, and in the end we have firm support and find security only in him. This is expressed in a most moving way in the last lines that were found at the side of Luther's deathbed. They are not the result of his theological research, but are a heartfelt expression of his experience of faith, to which all theology must submit: "Wir sein pettler. Hoc est verum" (We are beggars; this is the pure truth).[3]

What we have just said could easily lead to the misunderstanding that God should merely (or predominantly) be there to intervene when man finds himself confronted with the limits of his possibilities. Obviously Jesus was aware of this danger. He warns his disciples not to think about God only when they find themselves at an impasse; they should pray to God continuously and tirelessly. He tells a short story to illustrate this point.

"In a certain city there was a judge who neither feared God nor regarded man; and there was a widow in that city who kept coming to him and saying, 'Vindicate me against my adversary.' For a while he refused; but afterward he said to himself 'Though I neither fear God nor regard man, yet because this widow bothers me, I will vindicate her, or she will wear me out by her continual coming'" (Lk. 18,2-5).

There is no need to think of this widow as advanced in years. At that time girls were married at about fourteen, and the average life expectancy was far lower than today. After her husband's death the woman was totally unprotected. She had no one to represent her interests in a society in which only men had the final word. None of the disciples to whom Jesus told this story would have been surprised about the widow's lot. At most, one or other of them might have been reminded that the prophets of the past had already raised their voices against the injustices practiced against widows and orphans: "....seek justice, correct oppression; defend the fatherless, plead for the widow!" (Is. 1,17).

The widow Jesus tells us about only wants her rights. But it is obvious that she has nothing to give as a present to the judge, so that her case could be taken into consideration. The judge is "godless" and that means corrupt, bribable, autocratic, and only concerned about his own well being. It is not the widow's anger that brings him to his senses, but the desire to be left in peace.

Does God treat us as this judge treats the widow? Does he simply listen to prayer moodily or out of pure idleness?

Almost certainly Jesus's disciples did not get this from the parable. They would have understood the parable at once; God should not be turned to only in anxious and hesitant prayer; what is important is this helpless widow's *will to persevere*. Every request reaches God's ears and his heart if it is insistent and steadfast enough.

The final comments show that this lies at the center of the whole parable:

"Hear what the unrighteous judge says. And will not God vindicate his elect, who cry to him day and night? Will he delay long over them? I tell you, he will vindicate them speedily: Nevertheless, when the Son of Man comes, will he find faith on earth?" (Lk. 18,6-8).

In other words, if this blackguard of a judge is moved to capitulate before the persistence of a powerless woman, how much more will your incessant pleas soften *God's* heart! It is probable that this commentary does not go back to Jesus himself, but to the evangelist, because he was afraid that the comparison between the heartless judge and God would be too irreverent for his readers.

The last sentence (will the Son of Man find faith on earth?) also reflects the fear of the post-Easter community that the second coming will be further delayed. On the other hand, the evangelist emphasizes that God *is already* standing by his own, if only they believe constantly, and pray calmly. The parable aims at one thing, and this is shown in the introduction; "And he told them a parable, to the effect *that they ought always to pray and not lose heart" (Lk. 18,1).*

The actual theme of this story is the persistence in prayer (which of course presupposes persistence in belief), and not the answering of prayer. Jesus comes to terms with this in another parable, also found in Luke.

"And he said to them (the disciples; compare 11,1) 'Which of you who has a friend will go to him at midnight and say to him, 'Friend, lend me three loaves; for a friend of mine has arrived on a journey, and I have nothing to set before him'; and he will answer from within, 'Do not bother me; the door is now shut, and my children are with me in bed; I cannot get up and give you anything'? I tell you, though he will not get up and give him anything because he is his friend, yet because of his importunity he will rise and give him whatever he needs'" (Lk. 11,5-8).

This story of the importunate friend (which was probably originally handed down as a companion parable to the story of the persistent widow) is an illustration of Jesus's catechesis of prayer contained in Luke's gospel. After the disciples had watched Jesus at prayer, one of them asks him to teach them how to pray, and he gives the Lord's prayer to them (Lk. 11,1-4). After this he tells them the story of the importunate friend. This is to strengthen their trust that in turning to God the father, he will always have an open ear for their needs and requests. We can only understand the whole range of this parable when we visualize the conditions of life in Palestine at the time.

There was no bakery in the village. Every family had its supply of grain, and a part of this was ground and made into bread. That nothing was left of this in the evening was not surprising; neither was it surprising that acquaintances travelling through often asked for shelter when darkness was falling. As a rule a village house consisted of one inner room. The whole family's sleeping place was a platform raised above this. When darkness fell the door was locked with a strong beam spanning its width and fastened to the side posts. If the husband had to get up and strike a light the children would be restless, and wakened entirely when he pushed back the lock or the beam, inevitably making a noise. It is quite understandable why the householder made it clear to his neighbor that he could not fulfil his wish. On the other hand, he must have remembered that he would *certainly* have to give his *own* unexpected friends something to eat, because the law of friendship had priority over every personal consideration.

In this parable the householder seems to attach no importance to these arguments, nor does friendship seem to play any part. The only thing that moves him to give in is his neighbor's importunate behavior that borders on the outrageous. The situation is similar to that of the persistent widow. Like the unrighteous judge, the householder does not act out of any noble motive, but from purely selfish reasons. Both of them have had enough of listening to all this whining, they just want to be left in peace.

As in the parable of the persistent widow, Jesus ends the parable of the importunate friend with an image of less becoming more, of the small becoming greater:

"And I tell you, ask and it will be given you; seek, and you will find; knock, and it will be opened to you. For everyone who asks receives, and he who seeks finds, and to him who knocks it will be opened. What father among you, if his son asks for a fish will instead of a fish give him a serpent; or if he asks for an egg, will give him a scorpion? If you then, who are evil, know how to give good gifts to your children, how much more will the heavenly Father give the Holy Spirit to those who ask him?" (Lk. 11,9-14)

Jesus follows the same line in both parables. He not only wishes to encourage us to pray intensely, but also underlines the *necessity* of this intense prayer. The main accent in the story of the widow lies in being tireless and persistent in prayer, and in the parable of the importunate neighbor in being certain that the prayer will be heard.

Almighty God?

The main condition therefore for prayer being heard is steadfastness. Of course, we then silently assume that it does indeed lie in God's power to grant us everything we ask for.

Really everything? In his novella "The Grey Horse Rider" which appeared in 1888, Theodor Storm tells us how Hauke, master of the dike, stands wringing his hands at the bedside of his wife, who is at the point of death from childbed fever after the birth of her daughter:

"The doctor had been fetched from the town, he sat by the bed, felt her pulse, prescribed, and looked about hopelessly. Hauke shook his head: 'He can't help; only God can help!' He had counted upon his own Christianity, but there was something that held his prayer back. When the old doctor had gone, he stood at the window staring out into the wintery day, and while the sick woman cried out in her dreams, he clasped his hands together; he did not know himself whether it was out of silent devotion or whether it was only out of the monstrous fear of not losing his mind... 'Lord, my God' he cried 'Do not take her from me! You know I can't do without her!' Then it was as if he came to his senses, and he continued softly: 'I know well, you can't help every time as you want to, even you; you are all-wise, and you have to act according to your wisdom — O Lord, just speak to me through your breath!" [4]

His housemaid heard this, and she went round the whole district telling of his prayer, which seemed heresy to her; "he questioned God's omnipotence; what would a God be then without omnipotence?"

Today most Christians would most likely share the doubts of Hauke more than the indignation of his housemaid. Her view of God's omnipotence corresponds largely to that of the great theologians of the Middle Ages, who were influenced more by ancient Greek philosophy than the Bible. They conferred all the attributes expressed in "absolute being" onto God; that he is sufficient unto himself, that he does not suffer pain in our sense of the word, that he is immutable, and of course, *omnipotent.*[5]

But the authors of the Bible also speak of God's omnipotence, his power and his glory. The oldest depictions of God in the Hebrew Bible, *El Shaddai* (the almighty God of the mountains: Gen. 17,1 etc) and *El* (God: Gen 33,20 etc), imply that there are no limits to the rule of the Jahweh-God. His imperious word creates what he wills (Is. 55,10f), his strong arm stretches everywhere (Job. 39-39), and no one can escape from his power (Ps. 139). But it is said of the same God that he seeks the society of men, that he feels compassion for them — and above all — that he is completely *powerless* against human freedom (and there can be no question about this).

Besides, Israel never experienced God's rule as tyranny. There was always the fervent conviction that God used his overpowering force exclusively for the well being of his people. When they lived according to his instructions, he would free them from their oppressors and support them against their enemies. But as soon as they turned from the right path, he would bring them to their senses. According to the understanding of the Hebrew Bible, Jahweh never used his power in an

228

arbitrary way; his actions always sprang from concern for his people and their well being.

Naturally Jesus also believed that man is subordinate to God in all his activities and perceptions (See Mt. 5.45: "...for he makes his sun rise on the evil and on the good") But strangely enough he hardly ever speaks about this. Instead he constantly emphasizes in his proclamation that God's rule does not consist in the practice of power and violence, but in *the caring and loving devotion towards mankind* — here we remember the two parables of the shepherd and the lost sheep, the woman and the lost drachma, and the parable of the merciful father and his two sons (Lk. 15, 1-32). Jesus is not contradicting the message of his own Hebrew Bible. Rather he is putting its emphasis elsewhere.

For their part the evangelists expressly point out that the Son of God himself undergoes a satanic temptation to exercise worldly power (Lk. 4, 5-13). But it is not through material force but only through the power of his love that Jesus tries to alter the world and mankind. In so far as Jesus represents the "...image of the invisible God" (Col. 1,15), his behavior is the key to an appropriate understanding of belief in God as the "almighty father." God's omnipotence is also subordinate to his love. In other words, the word "almighty" does not require us to believe that God intervenes as men do to alter the course of worldly events. It is solely God's omnipotent love which fundamentally transforms a man.

Echo as Answer?

We are urged (Rom. 8,26) to ask, in the spirit of Jesus, what we should pray for, so that we can discover his all powerful love everywhere, accept and reciprocate it.

This, of course, does not mean that we should not turn entirely and completely to God in every day matters. As a child who requires visible signs of affection from its parents so that it can put their love into concrete form, we may and should ask God to support us in all our cares and needs, because he also communicates his love to us through temporal things. Jesus himself points to this when he names two requests in the same breath, the coming of the kingdom of God and asking for our daily bread.

However, many of those who pray could object or protest here. In spite of Jesus's assurance that God hears every single prayer, we frequently have the experience that our prayers remain unanswered. Just at the moment when we are waiting urgently for a sign from God, we often discover that God does not speak, he does not answer, he does not help. God is silent.

Can we or should we be content with the thought that God's silence can be traced back to a lack of persistence on our part? If we pour out our hearts before God, tell him of all our pain and unhappiness, and all this with a trust (almost bordering on despair) that he alone can help and that he will help — are we not behaving exactly like the persistent widow to the judge, or the importunate friend to his neighbor?

But instead of continuing with theoretical discussions, it would be better to turn our attention to the narrator of the two parables. We know that he did not limit himself simply to exhorting those around him to trust God completely and to subordinate themselves to his will. In his darkest hour he takes himself at his own word when, in fear of death, he begs God "Abba, father, all things are possible to thee; remove this cup from me; yet not what I will, but what thou wilt" (Mk. 14,36). He is expressing a particular request here, but at the same time he is asking the father to decide what is right from his point of view: "Now is my soul troubled. And what shall I say? 'Father, save me from this hour'? No, for this purpose I have come to this hour. Father, glorify thy name" (Jn. 12,27-28).

We can only speak of true prayer that corresponds to the spirit of Jesus if we are prepared, like him, to use words of unconditional trust in God that are yet subordinate to the will of God: "*Thy* will be done" (Mt. 6,10). We have to follow Jesus's example by leaving all human needs entirely in God's care, in firm trust that "....in everything God works for good with those who love him" (Rom. 8,28).

The question of prayer being heard then acquires a new horizon. The example of Christ wrestling with his God on the Mount of Olives shows that this God can reserve the right to refuse a specific petition. But *not granting* prayer does not signify *not hearing* it.

If God does not grant a request it means that we are again thrown back upon ourselves. We must try to come to grips with a situation we have prayed to be changed. Or rather *we must change ourselves*, so that we can receive the greater gift that lies behind God's refusal. Augustine expresses this in one of his letters: "The Lord, who often does not grant us what we want, is good, in that he gives us what we actually *should* want for our good."[6]

In concrete terms this means that God can hear a prayer although he does not grant it the request as we would hope. *A prayer is always heard when we have found a firm basis and a sure support in God.* An example may clarify this: if a sick person prays to be healed, he sees in his recovery the basic assumption for

231

a happy and fulfilled life. *That* is what his prayer aims at, even if he does not take it into account. If he really trusts in God's incomprehensible ways in spite of his illness, and so finds his way back to inner composure, he has achieved what he was *actually* praying for; his prayer has been heard. Whenever the objective fulfillment of prayer is missing, God puts our trust to the test: do you trust me that I can bring about your healing in another way than the one you wanted?

This thought is also at the basis of the interpretation of the parable of the importunate friend: "If you then, who are evil, know how to give good gifts to your children, how much more will the heavenly father give *the Holy Spirit* to those who ask him!" (Lk. 11,13). As Matthew's gospel shows in a parallel passage (Mt. 7,11) the Holy Spirit here is goodness as such. In other words, hearing a prayer consists in God granting to man what is beneficial to him.

In prayer that has not been answered our requests to God actually become questions of faith, which God then gives back to us: do you really believe that I have the broader viewpoint, the more extensive horizon, the widest perspective? Sometimes such belief almost exhausts all human possibilities. But the famous words of St. Therese of Lisieux show that it does not go beyond some souls: "My God, when you do not hear me, I love you even more!"[7]

"Come here, you Child Murderer!"

A further and more agonizing question is linked to prayers of request: why does God often not answer prayers that simply aim to protect the innocent from suffering? In his novel "Die Jerominkinder" (the Jeromin Children) Ernst Wiechert shows that this question threatens the very foundations of belief. A priest prays constantly to God to spare at least the children from a merciless and raging epidemic. But his prayer is unanswered and God remains silent. Finally in his despair the priest breaks the image of the crucifix to pieces and screams:

"Come here, you child murderer, and show your bloody hands! Show them to me so that I can dry them for you! Weren't the first born of Egypt and the children of Bethlehem enough for you then? And wasn't your own son enough? You nailed him to the cross to redeem us, but now you go on redeeming, and always on crosses, don't you? You needed these children too, seventy-one of them from ten villages, and even now it's a blessing that it wasn't seventy times seven." [8]

We can object to some of these accusations. Did God really wish for the death of his son, or did he not rather send him to lead the chosen people back to him, the God of the covenant? Do we not all too easily transfer our own responsibility onto God, when we encumber him with the results of our own guilty failures? A great deal of suffering is not caused by God, but by man, who abuses his freedom.

But such objections overlook the real problem. How can an almighty and just God look on when misery caused by other people falls on those who are not responsible for its causes? And why are innocent children among the victims of epidemics, starvation and natural catastrophes, which as a rule cannot be traced back to human failure but to causes that lie outside human power and control?

Here we have reached the nub of the question about God's justice and his omnipotence. If God does not prevent the suffering of the innocent, although that lies within his power, there can be no talk of divine justice and love. But if he cannot prevent it, his omnipotence is in question. Is God then not just and loving, as the Bible and preachers maintain? Or is he perhaps not almighty? Or do both points apply? The fact is that we often *do not feel, see and experience* God's omnipotence and justice just at the point where *according to our feelings* we should feel, see and experience them.

Why suffering? Why the suffering of the innocent? Why does God sometimes seem to turn a deaf ear to the prayers that, according to our opinion (and that means according to our sense of justice) he should fulfill *unconditionally*? We do not know. If someone who believes wants to be honest with himself and others, there is nothing else left to him but to admit that he does not know the answer to this agonizing question. This "not knowing" is essentially linked to the mysteriousness of God.

If we want to develop this thought further, we must do it in the knowledge that theological speculations can indeed lead to belief, but can never take its place, and that every theoretical discussion about the problem of pain falls far short of explaining every existential experience of pain and overcoming pain.

The sufferings of the innocent and God's silence indeed lie at the basis of Christian faith. But one all too easily forgets that God, even as he reveals himself, remains hidden and mysterious, incomprehensible and sublime above everything. The prophet Isaiah therefore calls him "the savior" in the same breath as he addresses him as "a God who hides thyself" (Is. 45,15). This is right, for when God speaks to man, he does not step out of his mystery, but gives himself to man as *mystery itself.*

One cannot take these statements of belief in the greatness, incomprehensibility and mystery of God seriously enough. Admittedly it is in man's make up to succumb to the temptation of wanting to see God's cards. Paul warns his fellow Christians in Corinth about this. " ....for we walk by faith, not by sight" (2 Cor. 5,7).

In "The Grey Horse Rider" Storm does not say any more than this; he merely puts it more simply. Elke, Hauke's daughter, cannot accept that her *own* daughter is mentally handicapped. One evening she says to her husband:

"'So we have actually been left alone.'

But Hauke shook his head: 'I love her, and she puts her little arms round me and presses herself to my breast; I wouldn't miss that for all the treasure in the world!'

His wife looked darkly before her. 'But why?'she said, 'how have I deserved this, a poor mother?'

'Yes, Elke, of course I have also asked this of him who alone knows; but you know too, the Almighty gives us humans no answer — perhaps because we would not understand it.'"

The most astute theologian could not add anything to this, even if he wanted to point to the practical lessons that could be drawn from it. (Theodor Storm does not reflect any more about this in his story). It is only when we are prepared to leave what is good for us entirely to God's discretion that we can live our faith completely. Our relationship towards prayers of asking also shows how far this attitude can be realized.

It now becomes clear what the parables of the persistent widow and the importunate friend are finally about, and that is boundless trust in God. This trust is the basic assumption of all requests and prayers if we are to pray in the spirit of Jesus.

Such unconditional trust in God can only be deepened if we accept it in our daily behavior. If God fails to answer a prayer, if he is silent and seems to withdraw, it is often a heavy cross to bear. But is there not the contrary experience that makes it possible for us to say: what would I be if I could not express myself in prayer? What would I be without a God I can hold on to? What would I be without my faith that sustains me?

Footnotes

Introduction

1. There is a key to theological terms at the end of this book.

2. G.Stemberger, "Der Talmud." Introduction, Texts, Comments. Munich, 1982. 211 (Taamit 5b-6a).

3. The genre of stories that teach is only found in Luke's gospel. Other examples: The Two Debtors (Lk. 7,41f); The Rich Corn Merchant (12,16-20); The Unassuming Guest (14,7-11).

4. Compare ch.8 in this book, "Jesus, a Poor Man, speaks about Money."

5. Examples of this: W.Kasper "Jesus der Christus," Mainz, 1974; the same author, "Der Gott Jesu Christi," Mainz, 1982: H. Thielicke, "Mensch sein - Mensch werden," outline of a Christian anthropology, Munich, Zürich, 1976.

Chapter 1

1. R.M.Rilke, "Die Aufzeichnung des Malte Laurids Brigge", Munich 1962 (dtv vol. 45) 168. Gide offers a similar thesis in his story "The Return of the Prodigal Son."

2. F.Kafka, "Heimkehr" in "Sämtliche Erzählungen," Frankfurt a. M. 1970.

3. Wajikra Rabba, V11, 6,9; Lexikon religioser Grundbegriff. Judentum, Christentum, Islam; Graz, Vienna, Cologne, 1987, 115.

Chapter 2

1. F.Kafka, "The Metamorphosis" in "Stories," 1904-1924, tr. J.A. Underwood. Macdonald and Co., London and Sydney, 1981. Ch. 1, 9.

2. F.Kafka, "Letter to my Father," tr. Jane Wilde.

3. E.Drewermann, "Wort des Heils - Wort der Heilung. Von der befreienden Kraft des Glaubens." Gespräche und Interviews, herausgegeben von B. Marz, vol.1. Düsseldorf 1988, 62. tr. Jane Wilde.

4. Berakhot, 2,3c; analogous to J.Jeremias, "Die Gleichnisse Jesu," Göttingen, 1965, 137f. tr. Jane Wilde.

5. Compare H.L.Strack/P. Billerbeck, "Kommentar zum Neuen Testament aus Talmud und Midrasch," vol. 1V/1: Exkurse zu einzelnen Stellen des Neuen Testaments, Munich, 1961, 484-500.

6. Sota 22a; Compare Strack/Billerbeck, 499.

7. R.Meyer, "Der Talmud. Ausgewählt, übersetzt und erklärt," Munich 1986, (Goldmann Klassiker, vol. 7571), 365 (Abot 1,3); the quotation to follow: G. Stemberger, "Der Talmud. Einführung, Texte, Erläuterungen," Munich 1982, 221 (Berakhot, 17a).

8. H.Böll, "Ansichten eines Clowns," Munich, 1972 (dtv. vol. 400) 250.

9. R.Meyer, "Der Talmud," 367 (Abot 1,15). For similar and even stricter parts of the Talmud ("he who learns in order to do nothing afterwards, it would be better if he had never been born") see H.L.Strack/P. Billerbeck, "Kommentar zum Neuen Testament aus Talmud und Midrasch," vol.1: "Das Evangelium nach

Matthäus," Munich,1965, 91f. Compare H. Kahlefeld, "Gleichnisse und Lehrstücke im Evangelium," vol.2, Frankfurt a. M. 1963, 16f.

10. Strack/Billerbeck, vol.1. 915-17.

11. F.M.Dostoevsky, "Crime and Punishment," Everyman's Library, J.M.Dent and Sons, 1941, 11.

12. Compare Thomas Aquinas, "Summa Theologiae" II-II, 1-2. To what follows compare O.H.Pesch, "Hinführung zu Luther," Mainz, 1982, 154-175.

13. M.Luther, "Adventspostille" (1522 to Mt. 21,1-9) from the Weimar edition, vol.10/1-2, 24; the following quotation; ebd. 24f; words in bold emphasis are the author's.

14. M.Luther, "Propositiones" from the Weimar edition, vol.7, 231.

15. H. Denzinger, "Kompendium der Glaubensbekenntnisse und kirchlichen Lehrentscheidungen"; verbessert, erweitet und ins Deutsche übertragen und unter Mitarbeit von. H. Hoping herausgegeben von P. Hünermann, Freiburg i. Br. Basle, Rome, Vienna, 1991, no. 1532 (from now on abbreviated to DH, followed by the marginal number used in the book).

16. T.Moser, "Gottesvergiftung," Frankfurt a. M. 1976, 43f; tr. Jane Wilde.

17. This comparison I owe to Ch. Wrembeck, "Königliches Hochzeitsmahl," in: "Geist und Leben" 64, (1991) 17-40; 27.

Chapter 3

1. Fyodor Dostoevsky, "The Brothers Karamazov," ch. 5, "The Grand Inquisitor." 255. tr. Constance Garnett. William Heinemann, London 1951. The following quotations from pp.256-7, 261, 264.

2. Erasmus of Rotterdam "Praise of Folly," Penguin classics, 1971. tr. Betty Radice, 162-3.

3. In what follows I pursue some thoughts that I expanded more fully elsewhere: see J.Imbach, "Himmelsglaube und Höllenangst; was wissen wir vom Leben nach dem Tod?" Munich, 1987, 44.

4. DH, 411.

5. Thomas Aquinas, "Summa Theologiae" Supplementum, q.14,a.3, in c.

6. J.B.Brantschen, "Hoffnung für Zeit und Ewigkeit. Der Traum vom wachen Christenmenschen," Freiburg, Basle, Vienna, 1992, 156.

7. ed. C.Selmer, "Navigation Sancti Brendani Abbatis" from early Latin manuscripts, Notre Dame, 1959. Quoted by D. Dieckmann in "Judas als Sündenbock; eine verhängnisvolle Geschichte von Angst und Vergeltung," Munich 1991, 42.

8. Augustine "Enchridion ad Laurentium, sive de fide, spe et caritate" cap.112, in "Patrologia latina," vol.40, 231-290; 284f.

9. see Diekmann for a résumé of this store of legends.

10. compare S.Brettle. "San Vincente Ferrer und sein literarischer Nachlaß," Münster, 1924, 41f.

11. ed. P.Wackernagel, "Das deutsche Kirchenlied von der ältesten Zeit bis zum Anfang des 17. Jahrhunderts," 5 vols. Leipzig, 1864-1877; vol. 2, 471.

12. This applies particularly to the writers of our century (except Paul Claudel, "The Death of Judas," 1935). Compare, amongst others; Nicos Kazantzakis, "The Last Temptation," 1955; Max Brod, "The Master," 1952; Walter Jens, "The Case of Judas," 1975; Luise Rinser, "Mirjam," 1983. See also J. Imbach, "Judas hat tausend Gesichter; zum Judasbild in der

Gegenwartsliteratur" in H.Wagner (ed) "Judas Ischariot. Menschliches oder heilsgeschichtliches Drama?" Frankfurt a. M. 1985, 91-143.

13. An example of such a curse formula is in "Patrologia latina," vol.87, 945-954.

Chapter 4

1. G.Bernanos, "The Diary of a Country Priest," Macmillan, N.Y., 1962. Tr: Pamela Morris.

2. J.W. von Goethe, Faust 1, verses 1222-27.

3. Th. Storm, "Der Schimmelreiter," Stuttgart 1959 (Reclams Universal-Bibliothek, vol. 6015/6016). Tr: Jane Wilde.

4. see J.Jeremias, "Die Gleichnisse Jesu," Göttingen, 1965, 146.

5. see Jeremias, 80-82.

6. G.Baudler, "Jesus im Spiegel seiner Gleichnisse; das erzählerische Lebenswerk Jesu - ein Zugang zum Glauben,"Stuttgart and Munich, 1988, 235.

7. W. Michaelis, "Die Gleichnisse Jesu," Hamburg, 1956, 48.

8. H.Kahlefeld, "Gleichnisse und Lehrstücke im Evangelium," vol. 1 Frankfurt a M. 1963, 58-62.

9. Baudler, 235

10. H.Fries, "Es bleibt die Hoffnung." Kirchenerfahrungen, Zürich, 1991, 47.

11. Codex to Canon Law, Canon 377, 1. Rome tries to get round the few dioceses that have a special legally established provision by appointing a coadjutor with right of succession (for example, in Chur in Switzerland).

12. Regulations of Ecclesiastical University Law, "sapientia christiana" of 15.4.1979, Art. 27, par. 2.

13. See W.Seibel, "Lehramt und Wissenschaftsfreiheit." Observations on a "Nihil Obstat" procedure in Stimmen der Zeit, 210, (1992) 685-692.

14. Dogmatic Constitution on the Church, "Lumen gentium," no.9.

15. Dogmatic Constitution on Divine Revelation, "Dei verbum," no.10.

Chapter 5

1. F.M.Dostoevsky, "The Brothers Karamazov," Heinemann, London 1951, 367.

Chapter 6

1. L.N.Tolstoy, Tales, "Two Old Men," Jarrold and Sons, London 1901. Tr: R. Nisbet Bain.

2. R.Meyer, "Der Talmud." Selections translated and explained, Munich 1986, (Goldmann Klassiker, vol.7571) 227f. The maxim is found in similar form in the (anonymous) letter of Aristeas (207), which could have been written between 130 and 100 B.C. Compare H.L.Strack/P. Billerbeck, "Kommentar zum Neuen Testament aus Talmud und Midrasch," vol.1: "Das Evangelium nach Matthäus," Munich, 1965, 460.

3. Examples, also of what follows, in Strack/Billerbeck, vol.1, 354-364.

4. Quoted by Strack/ Billerbeck, vol.1, 542.

5. Compare Lk. 9,52f, with Josephus Flavius, "Jüdische Altertümer," 20,6; the following episode, 18,3. For such pollution see Num.19,11-16.

6. See E. Lohse (ed.) "Die Texte aus Qumran; Hebräisch und Deutsch," Munich 1964, 180-225.

7. Patrologia latina, vol. 87, 952-954. Further examples, 945-952.

8. after J. Gnilka, "Das Matthäusevangelium," vol.2, Freiburg, Basle, Vienna, 1988, 372.

9. J.W. von Goethe, Faust, pt.1, verse 3415.

10. Egyptian Book of the Dead, ch. 123. Quoted by Gnilka, 373.

11. In greater detail in J.Imbach, "Kleiner Grundkurs des Glaubens," Düsseldorf, 1990, 170-179.

12. compare DH, 1351

13. Dogmatic Constitution on the Church, "Lumen gentium," no.16; DH 4140.

Chapter 7

1. Alberto Moravia, "La Noia."

2. Quoted in J. Jeremias, "Die Gleichnisse Jesu," Göttingen, 1965, 182. "The manuscript is from c. 50-100 A.D.; the story itself dates from 331 B.C. the terminus post quem" (ebd).

3. G.Stemberger, "Der Talmud," introduction, text, explanations. Munich 1987, 208 (Schabbat 153a).

4. See following chapter.

5. Stemberger, "Talmud," 208, (Schabbat 153a).

Chapter 8

1. The quotations that follow are from the English translation by Katherine Woods; "The Little Prince,"Harcourt Brace, N.Y., 1943.

2. E.Drewermann, "Das Eigentliche ist unsichtbar. Der kleine Prinz tiefenpsychologisch gedeutet," Freiburg i. Br. 1990, 21,35.

3. From Erich Fromm, "Haben oder Sein," Stuttgart, 1976. tr. Jane Wilde.

4. G. Bernanos, "Sermon of an Atheist on the Feast of the little Saint Therese." tr. Jane Wilde.

Chapter 9

1. Francis of Assisi, The Final Rule, (ch.1) in Works, vol. 201, Zürich 1979, 37-44; 38.

2. Francis of Assisi, The Early Rule, (ch. 22) from Works.

3. Francis of Assisi, Fioretti, (no.23) from Works.

4. J.W. von Goethe, Faust 1, verses 1112-1117.

5. See Strack/Billerbeck, vol. 1, 608-610

6. I.B.Singer, "The Penitent," Jonathan Cape, 1984, 83.

7. The Legend of the Three Companions" (no.23) in: O.Karrer (ed.) "Franz von Assisi, Legenden und Laude," Zürich 1945, 143-290; 180.

Compare nos. 55 and 59, also the Fioretti, no.9.

Chapter 10

1. The Childhood Gospels of Pseudo Matthew, 14,1. Translation from L. Moraldi (ed.) "Apocrifi del Nuovo Testamento, vol. 1. Turin, 1971, 199-239; 217.

2. M.T.Cicero, Pro. C. rabirio perduellionis reo, Cap. V, 16 in Opera, vol.11/1, ed. I.C. Orellius, Turici, 1854, 650.

3. S. Kierkegaard, *The Moment*

4. Compare H. Kahlefeld, "Gleichnisse und Lehrstücke im Evangelium," vol.1, Frankfurt a. M. 1963, 149-170; J. Gnilka, "Das Mattäusevangelium," vol.2, Freiburg, Basle, Vienna, 1988, 355-365.

Naturally there are some insertions and alterations in Luke's gospel, which are determined by his interpretation of the parable (19, 12-27). According to Luke, the main character is a nobleman who travels to a distant country to receive a kingdom. His fellow countrymen send an embassy after him to prevent this, but they are not successful. After his return the new king calls the ten servants to account for the money he has entrusted to them. Finally he slays the enemies who tried to prevent his coronation. Here Luke works in some facts from the Jewish historian Josephus Flavius ("Jewish Antiquities", 17,17). We have been told of the following events from the Jewish war (2,2): in 4 B.C. an embassy from Judaea and Samaria tried to prevent the coronation of Herod's detested son Archelaus, but in spite of this, he was recognized, and after his return from Rome, he caused a blood bath among the leading citizens of Jerusalem. The events are changed in Luke's version of the parable, and applied to Jesus allegorically. The king becomes a nobleman, who stands for Christ; the servants are the baptized; the religious leaders who oppose Jesus are disguised as the embassy. Finally, the blood bath either refers to the Last Judgement, or, which is more likely, to the destruction of Jerusalem.

5. For more details see; J.Imbach, "Daß der Mensch ganz sei. Vom Leid, vom Heil und vom ewigen Leben in Judentum, Christentum und Islam," Düsseldorf, 1991, 65-75.

6. J.B.Metz, "Jenseits bürgerlicher Religion. Reden über die Zukunft des Christentums," Munich and Mainz, 1980, 25f

7. Francis of Assisi, The Final Rule (sealed on Nov 29 1223 by Pope Honorius III), ch.2 in Works, vol.21.

Chapter 11

1. In the first part of this chapter I sum up some thoughts that I have already dealt with elsewhere; compare J.Imbach, "Kleiner Grundkurs des Glaubens," Düsseldorf, 1990, 125-136.

2. From B.Brecht, "Mother Courage and her Children."

3. Martin Luther, "Tischreden," vol. 5. No. 5677.

4. from Th. Storm, "Der Schimmelreiter."

5. For more details see: H. Frohnhofen, "Ist der christliche Gott allmächtig? Zur aktuellen Diskussion über ein altes Bekenntnis" in Stimmen der Zeit, 210, (1992) 519-528.

6. Augustine, Letter 31,1 (to Paulinus and Theresia) in Patrologia latina, vol.33, 121.

7. Quoted by H. Schaller, "Das Bittgebet. Eine theolog.ische Skizze," Einsiedeln,1979, 185.

8. E. Wiechert, "Die Jerominkinder," Munich, 1954, 220.

Special Terms

Allegory:

Narrative description of a subject under guise of another, but having similarities to it. Comes from the Greek *alla agoreuin* = a way of saying something else.

Apocalypse:

The expectation of the approaching end of the world in early Judaism and early Christianity. The apocalyptic movement was expressed in numerous documents (e.g. the Apocalypse of John).

Apocrypha:

Manuscripts which reveal many similarities with the books of the Old and New Testaments, but which were not included in the Bible (i.e. the Gospel of Thomas, the Protoevangelium of James). Their authors wanted to fill in the gaps of the biblical accounts (e.g. Jesus's childhood) or to replace them with other writings.

Babylonian Captivity; Babylonian Exile:

Lasted from 597-586 BC when Nebuchadnezzar II conquered Jerusalem and deported the Jews to Babylon. They returned under Cyrus II in 538 BC.

Day of Jahweh:

The prophets thought of this primarily as a future judgment of God over Israel which would send the people forth enlightened and revenged upon their enemies (Mal. 3,2; Zech. 12,1-20). Later apocalyptic conceptions of "the day of the Lord" are in agreement with the prophetic visions that the changes expected will lead to improvement in *this* world. All injustice will be overcome so that peace and justice will henceforth rule among men. Later Jahweh's day of judgment became more and more linked to the coming *end of the world* (Dan. 9,26; 12,13) when "one like a Son of Man" (Dan. 7,13f) will appear. Jesus shared this view, and the early Christian church took it over, at the same time modifying it. The Son of Man expected now becomes identified with Christ, whose Parousia (second coming) was thought to be imminent.

Gemara: see Talmud.

The Hebrew Bible:

Corresponds to the Old Testament scriptures canonically recognized by the Roman Catholic church with the exception of the books of Judith, Tobit, First and Second Book of the Maccabees, Wisdom of Solomon, Sirach, and Baruch; The Greek additions to the Book of Esther (1,1a-r; 3,13a-g; 4,17a-z; 5,2a-b; 8,12a-v; 10,3a-k), and Daniel (3,24-90; 13; 14). The reformed churches on the other hand, hold to the Hebrew Bible with regard to the first (Old) Testament.

Midrash:

Means research, teaching, and is a commentary on part of the Hebrew scriptures. In contrast to the *Mishnah* (see Talmud) the Midrash always interprets a verse or a passage from part of the Bible, which is used as a text to be read or preached during service. The numerous interpretations of rabbinical and Talmudic Judaism until the beginning of the Middle Ages belong to Midrash literature.

Parable: See Simile.

Parousia:

Christ's second coming. See Day of Jahweh.

Proselyte:

A gentile who converted to Judaism in ancient times.

Qumran:

A district at the northwest end of the Dead Sea. At the time of Jesus it was the home of a Jewish religious movement, the so-called Qumran community which had set itself apart from official Judaism. Its monastic-like settlement was destroyed by the Romans in 68 AD. In 1947 several manuscripts were found in caves, amongst them the rule of the order and books of the Hebrew Bible.

Rabbi:

In the Talmud and New Testament the word means "master" or "teacher." The title became an honored one which was carried by the Palestinian teachers of the law from the end of the first century AD. The great Jewish teachers were all called rabbis. The Jewish heads of the community were called rabbin, and their position corresponded somewhat to that of a vicar or preacher in the protestant churches.

Simile:

A comparison, principally in the form of a story. Jesus's actual similes are concerned with everyday events (e.g. the woman who loses her drachma and then cleans out her whole house, see Lk. 15,8-10); from this the kingdom of God and God's behavior is inferred, or man's destiny and his correct dealings. A parable, on the other hand, is a simile in which a single and not an everyday event is depicted. Related to the parable we have the literary genre of stories that teach or set examples. They show us either models of actions that should be imitated, or examples that shock us, and so are a stimulus for practical behavior (i.e. the story of the Good Samaritan, Lk. 10,25-37). See also allegory.

Synoptist:

One of the evangelists Matthew, Mark, and Luke, whose gospels correspond often and extensively to one another and therefore form a *synopsis*.

Talmud:

Literally "the Study." It is a collection of laws and religious records of post-biblical Judaism, which developed during the time c. 200 BC to roughly 500 AD. In the outer form of the text one distinguishes between the *Mishnah* ("repetition," which is the teaching of the fathers, learnt by being repeated sentence by sentence) and the *Gemara* (completion of the teaching or commentaries by later teachers). There are two versions of the Talmud which are called after their district; the *Palestinian* and the *Babylonian Talmud*. Mishnah sentences are quoted according to chapter (Roman numerals) and paragraphs (Arabic numerals). The parts of the *Gemara*, however, are quoted according to leaves and sides of the manuscripts, *a* depicting the facing page, *b* the reverse. For example:

Chagiga II.2 = Palestinian Talmud, tract Chagiga (=ceremonial offering) Mishnah, ch. 2. par.2.

Shabbat 30a.b =tract Shabbat (the Sabbath) Gemara, leaf 30, facing and reverse side.

If there is a j before a tract (e.g. j Shabbat) it means the quotation has come from the Palestinian (i.e., Jerusalem) version of the Talmud.

Torah:

Hebrew word for "instruction" or "law." In a narrower sense in ancient Judaism it signifies the five Books of Moses (Genesis, Exodus, Leviticus, Numbers, Deuteronomy); in a wider sense the whole of the Old Testament, and frequently also the whole of Jewish religious Law.

DATE DUE

List of Parables

The following list corresponds to the order in which Jesus's parables are dealt with in this book. The additions in parentheses point to parallel passages in the other evangelists.

1. The Substance of Jesus's Preaching
The Prodigal Son: Lk. 15,11-32
The Shepherd and the Lost Sheep: Lk. 15,4-7. (Mt. 18,12-14)
The Woman and the lost Drachma: Lk. 15,8-10

2. God Knows No Love that can be Bought
Laborers in the Vineyard: Mt. 20,1-16
The Man with Two Sons: Mt. 21,28-32
The Pharisee and the Publican: Lk. 18, 9-14
The Modest Guest: Lk. 14,8-11
The Two Debtors: Lk. 7,41-42

3. Damned for all Eternity?
The Unfruitful Fig Tree: Lk. 13,6-9 (Mk. 11,12-14)
The Rebellious Tenants: Mk. 12,1-9 (Mt. 21,33-41 ; Lk. 20,9-16)
The Fish Net: Mt. 13,47-50
The Way to the Judge: Mt. 5,25-26 (Lk. 12,58-59)

4. Of Expectations, of Disappointments, and of Success
The Sower: Mk. 4,3-8 (Mt. 13,3-8; Lk. 8,5-8)
The Growing Seed: Mk. 4,26-29 (see Mt. 13,24-30; The Wheat and the Weeds)
The Mustard Seed: Mk. 4,30-32 (mt. 13, 31-32; Lk. 13, 18-19)
The Leaven and the Flour: Lk. 13,20-21 (Mt. 13,33)
The Wheat and the Weeds Mt.13,24-30 (see Mk, 4,26-29 The Growing Seed)

251

5. The Bridge upon which Man and God Meet
The Debtor Servant: Mt. 18,23-35

6. Love Alone is Crucial
The Good Samaritan: Lk. 10,25-37 (see Mk. 12,28-34; Mt. 22,34-40)
The Last Judgment: Mt. 25,31-46

7.To Gain the Whole World and Lose One's Life?
The Moody Children: Mt. 11,16-19 (Lk. 7, 31-35)
The Rich Man and Lazarus: Lk. 16,19-31
The Watchful Householder: Mtt. 24,43-44 (Lk. 12,39-40; see Mk. 13,35)
The Guest without a Wedding Garment: Mt. 22,11-14
The Sprouting Fig Tree: Mk. 13,28-29 (Mt. 24,32-33; Lk. 21, 29-31)
The Wise and Foolish Maidens: mt. 25,1-12
The Servants on the Watch: Mk. 13,33-37 (see Mt. 25, 13-15; 24,42; Lk. 21,36; 19,12-13; 12,40; 12,38)
The Servant put to the Test: Mt. 24,45-51 (Lk. 12,42-46)

8. Jesus, a Poor Man, Speaks about Money
The Rich Corn Merchant: Lk. 12,16-20
The Treasure in the Field: Mt. 13,44
The Priceless Pearl: Mt. 13,45-46
The Marriage Feast: Lk. 14,16-24 (Mt. 22,1-14)

9. Decisions for Life?
The Unclean Spirit: Mt. 12,43-45 (Lk. 11,24-26)
Building a Tower: Lk. 14,28-30
Waging War: Lk. 14,31-32

10. At the Foot of the Cross
The Parable of the Talents: mt. 25,14-30 (Lk. 19,12-27)
The Dishonest Steward: Lk. 16,1-8

11 "We are Beggars"
The persistent Widow: Lk. 18,2-8
The importunate Friend: Lk. 11,5-8

List of Names